GREEK ORATIONS

GREEK
ORATIONS

LYSIAS
ISOCRATES
DEMOSTHENES
AESCHINES
HYPERIDES

AND

LETTER OF PHILIP

ꓕ

EDITED, WITH AN INTRODUCTION, BY

W. ROBERT CONNOR

ANN ARBOR PAPERBACKS
THE UNIVERSITY OF MICHIGAN PRESS

First edition as an Ann Arbor Paperback 1966
Copyright © by The University of Michigan 1966
All rights reserved
Library of Congress Catalog Card No. 66-17355
Published in the United States of America by
The University of Michigan Press and simultaneously
in Toronto, Canada, by Ambassador Books Limited
Manufactured in the United States of America

Acknowledgment is gratefully made to the following publishers
for permission to quote copyrighted material:
Harvard University Press, Loeb Classical Library: Hyperides
Funeral Oration, from C.O. Burney's *Minor Attic Orators II*
(1954); Against Ctesiphon (excerpts), from C.D. Adams' *The
Speeches of Aeschines* (1919); Isocrates To Philip (excerpts),
from Isocrates, *Orations,* translated by George Norlin (1928).
Clarendon Press, Oxford: Olynthiac II, Philippic I, Philippic II,
De Corona (excerpts), from A.W. Pickard-Cambridge's *Demos-
thenes Orations.*

PA
3481
.C6

PREFACE

The purpose of this volume is to make available to a wider public some of the speeches of an age of spectacular rhetoric. Athens in the fourth century B.C. saw what might be considered the world's greatest age of oratory and witnessed an unparalleled development in the techniques for public address. Yet the literary accomplishment of this period cannot be isolated from politics, nor the study of Aeschines, Isocrates, Demosthenes, and the other orators from an investigation of the political and social issues of their day. Except perhaps for Isocrates none of these men ever thought of himself primarily as a literary figure. They were citizens, advocates, politicians, and, in occasional moments of idealism, statesmen. Thus, to deal with their work we must deal with their environment, the city they lived in, the rivals and opponents they attacked, and the problems they struggled with.

For the period of the greatest activity and greatest perfection of Greek oratory this environment is summed up in one great confrontation: Athens vs Macedon. Implicit in it are countless sequels and corollaries: the juxtaposition of city with kingdom, of assembly with autocrat, of pro-Athenian democrats with pro-Macedonian oligarchs, of factions within the city, of contrary assessments of the king of Macedon, of personal rivalries among the orators.

The best way to understand the background to these conflicts is to study the orators themselves, for they are not only the primary source for this period of Greek history, they also bring the era to life—not through the learned dispassion of the historian but with the passion and involvement of men who have themselves struggled with the problems of which they speak. For this reason the following pages keep commentary to a minimum and the focus narrowed on a relatively short period, the twenty years or so in which Philip of Macedon established his hegemony over the Greeks. To be sure, understanding these years requires some realization of how the Athenians thought about themselves, their neighbors, and their past. Although the Lysianic *Funeral Oration* was written long before Philip's entrance into Greek history, it is included to provide a wider historical perspective and to help explain the Athenians' attitudes and the background to later events. Similarly, a diplomatic communique from Philip's court, embodying the techniques of Attic rhetoric though not strictly an oration, provides an indispensable opportunity to see the Macedonian side of the dispute. For the sequel to Philip's victory over Athens and Thebes the speeches of Aeschines and Demosthenes at the trial of Ctesiphon are a principal source and Hyperides' *Funeral Oration* a fitting conclusion. Thus, the volume comprehends approximately seventy years from roughly 395 to 322 B.C. and includes all three major genres of oratory—the speech before the assembly (demagoric), the court room case (dicanic), and the ceremonial address (epideictic).

In preparing this volume I have received valuable help and advice from P. H. Burian, H. D. Cameron, Helen Connor, J. V. A. Fine, J. A. Hanson and from many friends in Ann Arbor, Michigan.

Princeton, New Jersey

CONTENTS

INTRODUCTION

Many ages looking across the years to Greece of the fourth century B.C. have found their own image reflected back to them. Cicero, three hundred years removed from the struggles of Macedon and Athens, saw Mark Antony as a latter-day Philip of Macedon and hoped that he himself would be a second, more prolific and more fortunate, Demosthenes. Late in the fifteenth century Bessarion, patriarch of Constantinople, issued a Latin translation of Demosthenes' First Olynthiac oration as part of the ecumenical effort of his day: the attempt to unite Eastern and Western Christendom against the rising power of the Turk. The earliest English translation of Demosthenes, whose title page proclaims it "most nedeful in these dangerous dayes of all them that love their Countries libertie," appeared in 1570, when a new Philip menaced Queen Elizabeth's England. Early in the eighteenth century some "eminent hands" in Britain, including George Granville and other leading politicians, produced a translation of the *Philippics* and *Olynthiacs* with the design, as Dr. Johnson put it, "of turning the thunder of Demosthenes upon the head of Lewis" XIV of France. After World War I, Clemenceau returned to his homeland, after a desperate effort in America to hold together the alliance that had brought victory but could not secure the peace, and wrote a biography of a Demosthenes in whom he found much of Washington, Lincoln, and more than a little of himself. Today, when the freedom and sometimes the very existence of smaller states are so often threatened by powers great in area, centralized in control, and ambitious in intent the apparent parallel in Athens' confrontation with Macedon will not be overlooked.

Yet, nothing can mislead like analogy. The superficial comparison of age to age, far from enlightening the student of history serves often only to confuse or delude. Indeed, the Athens of Demosthenes' own day may provide a notable example of the dangers of reliance on deceptive historical likenesses. The fourth-century orators knew and frequently alluded to the history of the preceding century, though their impressions are often blurred by the romantic light in which speeches like the Lysianic *Funeral Oration* presented the events. The speakers of this time refer to the fifth century not simply as a source for allusions and historical parallels, but as a means for intuiting their own period. Contemporary politics appears as a degenerate repetition of ancient history: Philip is a small scale, although despicably clever, re-creation of the Great King of Persia; Athens is once again Destiny's chosen instrument to stop the barbarian intrusion on the city-states; new Marathons await her if she will only be bold and firm. Many a politician, relaxing in these dreams of cyclical magnificence, no doubt quietly delighted in the thought that in his time too prestige, personal profit, and public benefaction could be combined into a Themistoclean grandeur.

Much of the assurance and some of the strange silences of Attic oratory in the fourth century can be explained by the speakers' feeling that the problem of the rise of Macedon was essentially the old problem of Persia with a few new variants. The same difficulty clearly called for the same solution. Demosthenes, for example, seems never to doubt that Philip was out for the destruction of Athens, would support her enemies even if she did nothing to provoke him, and would at every opportunity inflict on her the most wretched of his devices of oppression. Convinced that Philip was a new barbarian despot Demosthenes pays little attention to Macedonian interests and objectives, and his speeches contain surprisingly little analysis of Philip's motives, except the untroubled assertion that Philip was out to conquer the world. To judge from his speeches Demosthenes never doubted this assessment of Philip and anyone who did was to him a fool or hireling.

An aged and feeble Isocrates was one who dared to disagree. His *Letter to Philip*, published in his ninetieth year, must have seemed to many of its readers the hackneyed restatement of a theme exhausted by generations of epideictic oratory, the senile rantings of an impractical mind, the vicarious courage of a theoretician too timid ever to face a Greek assembly. The suggestion that Philip should lead a crusade of Greeks against the king of Persia was clearly unrealistic and could be dismissed at once—except that it turned out to be a prediction of what actually happened some twenty years later under Philip's son, Alexander the Great. However foolish Isocrates may have seemed, whatever silly idealism he indulged in, his mind could recognize the pattern of the future and adapt to it. Younger and more practical men lived in a fantasy world of clichés and twisted analogies which they called "reality."

The exoneration of Isocrates' policy began just at the time of his death. His last published work is a letter congratulating Philip on his victory over Athens and Thebes at Chaeronea in 338 B.C. Only a few days later, aware, active, flourishing to the very end, ninety-four years old, Isocrates died. The Athens of the day was, as usual, too distracted to pay much attention to her old adviser. The foreboding and outright terror that had preceded the battle gave way in the aftermath of Philip's victory to mingled awe and mystification. Philip's vindictive zeal against Athens, so lavishly promised by some orators, did not materialize. Thebes was punished, but Athens spared, deferred to, honored. The conqueror, supposedly bent on the destruction of all Athens stood for, was offered and gratefully received honorary Athenian citizenship. Philip had become beyond any challenge a Greek and an Athenian, and in a matter of months undertook the leadership of a Hellenic league in the preparations for the invasion of the Persian empire.

What Isocrates had clearly recognized Demosthenes too had glimpsed. Isocrates compliments; Demosthenes insults; but both use the same means. The fulsome old-fashioned mythic genealogies that trace Philip's ancestry back to Heracles, that survey the services of his ancestors to the Greek world, that enjoin on Philip a similar philhellenic policy are but the expressions of Isocrates' realization that Philip wanted, demanded, to be a Greek. Demosthenes' famous vulgarity:

> He is not only no Greek, nor a relative of any Greeks; he's not even a barbarian from any decent place. He is a damn Macedonian from a country where you could never even buy a good slave.
>
> (*Philippic* III §31)

stung in the same way that Isocrates flattered. Philip was not content to be a barbarian; he wanted to be a Greek. The man who as a hostage spent several years of his youth watching Epaminondas and Pelopidas in Thebes, who once in power called the leading Greek intellectuals of the day to his court, who invited Aristotle to tutor his son, whose chancery conducted his foreign correspondence with the fictions of Greek diplomacy and with the rhetoric of Greek oratory was not a man unmoved by the attractions of Hellenism. After full consideration is given to the political, economic, strategic reasons behind the invasion of Asia, this factor retains its importance: Philip wanted to be a Greek, and the leadership of a Greek expedition against the ancestral enemy of Hellas was the visible expression and fulfillment of this desire.

The submission of Athens to Macedon after the battle of Chaeronea in 338 B.C. or her failure to free herself from Macedon some sixteen years later in the Lamian War was long regarded as the termination of Greek history. The age that followed was dismissed or disparaged. Although the folly and narrowness of this view is now widely recognized, the feeling that Greek culture in the Hellenistic age was somehow in decline still lingers on. If anything, the contrary is the case. The late fourth and the third centuries may be viewed as periods of world-shaking explosions of Hellenism, which brought the Greek language, Greek literature, Greek political organization, Greek attitudes to areas that, however much contact they might have had with Greece before, had never been deeply affected by her culture. The first tremor of this explosion is the confrontation between Philip of Macedon and Athens and the other city-states to his south. What brought these powers face to face was not some sickness or decay within Greek civilization that, like a vacuum, drew Philip on, but the exact opposite: the vital and attractive power of a group of states which had achieved a political and intellectual existence that, for all its shortcomings, was infinitely superior to anything that portion of the world had known for a millennium. It was not the weakness of Greece that drew Philip on, but the strength of a culture he could not help but admire. The combination of sensuosity and intellect, of individual freedom and corporate order, of beauty and manliness which Pericles praised, which modern man begrudgingly admires, which the Renaissance unabashedly hoped to re-create, which countless cities in Egypt, the Levant, and the far reaches of Asia struggled throughout the Hellenistic period to embody, converted one of its earliest and one of its most important devotees in Philip of Macedon.

It is precisely this philhellenism that made Philip dangerous. A barbarian power in Macedon, even if naturally unsympathetic to the Greek states, could perhaps be held off, as Persia once had been, and in time a compromise arranged. Athens would have had to surrender, or at least to modify her territorial claims in the Thraceward regions, some agreement on free passage through the Hellespont would have to be made, and some suitable dividing line in northern Greece sketched out. But a modus vivendi was possible, especially as long as a hostile Persia threatened both barbarians in the north and Greeks in the south. A Macedon that thought herself a part of Greece, however, was a greater menace. Such a country would be likely to meddle in Hellenic affairs, would disarm opposition by professing friendship, and would insist on a voice in the assemblies of the Greeks. It would not be content with anything less than full Hellenism, and would not, therefore, be excluded from the original Hellenic organization, the Delphic Amphictyony. Admiring Hellenism it would be drawn into Hellas, disrupting, displacing, disarraying the world it esteemed so highly.

Demosthenes, always a man to intensify a narrow truth into brilliant rhetoric, could see this much. That this disruption might be unavoidable, that it could be beneficial, or that intransigent opposition might make

6

its effects worse, were not thoughts for him. He knew
for sure that Macedon threatened the order of the Greek
world and the primacy of Athens, and on this certainty
he built an eloquence that the world has never been
able to forget. Born into a prosperous middle class, educated not in the platitudinous liberal humanism of Isocrates but in the exacting technical specialization of the
post-Peloponnesian War orators, Demosthenes, even in
his most empassioned moments, is profoundly conventional. He makes few innovations in the form of ancient
oratory but raises to a new level what has been trans-
mitted to him. His speeches contain few original ideas,
but express and apply the accepted wisdom of the day
with what Longinus called "his unapproachable vehemence and power." What distinguishes him from his
lesser contemporaries—from Demades, Lycurgus, Di-
narchus, even from Aeschines and Hyperides—is his
singleness of mind, his ability to pursue his quarry with
unabated persistence, through all involutions and dis-
tractions, surmounting all obstacles, rejecting all compromise, despising all weakness until the emotions he
seeks "come alive in the listener's soul."

Philip was such a quarry, and Demosthenes made
him the obsession of the age. No problem could be
raised, no meeting adjourned without his name on worried lips. And from the fear came the reality. Every
speech which drew attention to Philip's power further
increased it. The constant discussions of his importance
and his interest in Greek affairs made it natural that he,
to Demosthenes' horror, should in 338 B.C. be called into
Greece to settle the Amphictyonic dispute with Amphissa. The resulting calls for alliance against Macedon
attracted Philip's attention to Athens and Thebes and
stimulated his efforts to divide city against city and
faction against faction. Whatever Philip's intention when
he responded to the Amphictyonic call to intervene in

the affair of Amphissa, the consternation and preparations of Athens must have encouraged him to seek a military solution to his disagreements with her.

Demosthenes' policies were thus, despite themselves, self-defeating. His every effort to block Philip served only to draw him closer and at last, at Chaeronea, to risk a provocation that would have brought Philip, if he were really the man Demosthenes thought he was, to destroy Athens. Instead, the city lived on to see the changes Demosthenes so much feared and to do what he had never been able to advise her to do, to adapt to them.

After this, the old age passes quickly. There is a gesture or two more: Demosthenes' final few years of influence, his most perfect speech, the oration *On the Crown,* a justification of his policy that will move men as long as they know the mingled pride and shame in the words "national honor," and the fatal eighteen months that saw the death of Alexander, his tutor Aristotle, and his great opponent, Demosthenes. Then a final, desperate blow: in the siege of Lamia, a hill town near Thermopylae, the attempt of Athens to free herself from Macedon in a short futile war. A new age of Greece begins, in which science, learning, poetry, art, the Greek language, even the reluctant city-states find a new vitality and a new power. One thing, and perhaps one thing alone, is missing, the oratorical passion of the age of Philip and Demosthenes. Hyperides' speech written for the funeral of those Athenians who fell in the Lamian War is the last monument of Attic eloquence. After that the technical excellence of Greek rhetoric is never doubted, its methods are refined and categorized and elaborated, barbarians from Italy learn and are changed in Greek rhetorical schools, but the passionate conviction that the spoken word can inform the act and transform the mind is never found in Greece again.

THE FUNERAL ORATION OF LYSIAS

INTRODUCTION

The first and last speeches in this book can be considered companion pieces marking the beginning and the end of a major period of the history of Greece. Both are epideictic (display or ceremonial) orations written for state funerals of Athenians who had died in military service. The first speech commemorates the casualties of the Corinthian War (395–87 B.C.) in which Athens, just recovering from her defeat in the Peloponnesian War, had once again taken arms against Sparta. This time, however, she was joined by her old enemies, Thebes and Corinth, who could themselves no longer endure Sparta's arrogance. The *Funeral Oration* of Hyperides at the end of this volume pays tribute to the Athenians who resisted Macedon in the Lamian War (323–22 B.C.), Athens' last major challenge to the Macedonians. The two speeches thus serve not only to delimit the period of Athens' final struggle for the hegemony of Greece, but also to record some of the changes in attitude, belief, and expression that took place in three-quarters of a century.

The epideictic genre has as its goal not so much success in arguing a point or convincing an audience as the proper ordering of an occasion by the expression of fitting sentiments. Its excellence is decorum, not originality. The speeches of this genre, including some of the most famous monuments of ancient oratory, such as Pericles' Funeral Oration in the second book of Thucydides, are elegant, formal, and, in the best sense of the word, conventional. It is a form where perfection of style, purity of language, and felicity of expression are the highest goods. In the *Funeral Oration* Lysias' writing is, for instance, far more antithetical and ornate than in any of his other thirty or so speeches. In fact, this,

9

and a few other peculiarities, have led some scholars to doubt that the oration is really his. Yet these same scholars often praise Lysias' ability to adapt his style to the speaker and to the occasion and concede that no explicit doubts were raised about the authenticity of the oration in antiquity. The case for Lysias' authorship is strong, but in any event the speech was surely known and admired in the fourth century B.C. and, even if it were not by Lysias, could safely be taken as a representative of one important style of oratory and one interesting view of past history and contemporary events in an important period of Greek history.

In comparison with some of the speeches that follow no one would claim for this oration a great originality or individuality. But for the historian this is perhaps its greatest value, for its very conventionality suggests the way a resident of Athens in the fourth century might have looked upon his city. The modern critical historian could not, of course, accept this speech as adequate history, but the sentiments, the romance, the fervor, and the patriotism of the Athenian citizen are all present, expressed as he himself would want them expressed.

The translation adopted here is by John Gillies, a gentleman historian of the late eighteenth century who, at the expense of a minute accuracy, managed to capture more of the flavor of the oration's style than any other translator. His renderings of Lysias and of Isocrates' *Panegyricus* can be criticized as occasionally archaic and inexact, but they possess one rare and redeeming virtue: they invite the reader to read aloud and they remind him at every turn that he is dealing not with the treatise or the text book but with the spoken and living word.

———

Proem
§§1–3

[1] If it were within the reach of eloquence to do justice to the merit of those who lie here interred, the state, doubtless, would be blameable in allowing to the orators only a few days for their preparation. But since it is altogether impossible to compose a discourse ade-

quate to so glorious a theme, I must rather admire the penetration of the magistrates, who, by assigning a short time for the execution of a task which could never be completely accomplished, have thus endeavoured to save the reputation of the speakers, and to cover them from a multitude of reproaches. [2] It is my ambition, therefore, to rival, not the glory which your warriors have acquired, but the eloquence with which your orators have displayed it. The actions of the former afford a subject of panegyric which all the praises of the latter can never fully exhaust; in every age, over seas and land, wherever mankind, subject to calamity and affliction, stand in need of tender sympathy and generous assistance, the virtues of the humane and the brave will be admired; their exploits will be recorded, and their name and glory will remain. [3] But before I endeavor to do justice to such as have lately aspired at so distinguished a renown, I must, according to custom, relate the ancient dangers of our forefathers, not drawing my information from written record, but from venerable traditionary fame, treasured in the heart and memory of every good citizen. It is the duty of all mankind to be mindful of our ancestors, to celebrate them with odes, to extol them with panegyrics, to honour them especially on such occasions as the present, that by praising the actions of the dead they may excite the virtues of the living.

[4] The Amazons, daughters of Mars, and inhabiting the banks of the Thermodon, were of old the only people in all those countries who wore armour of steel. They were the first who mounted on horseback, by which they gained the double advantage in war, of overtaking the enemy in their flight, and of eluding their pursuit. Having thus overcome by education the weakness of nature, they were estimated rather by their courage than by their sex, and were deemed to excel men

Past accomplishments of Athens §§4–66

i. Mythological period §§4–20

more in the vigour of their minds, than they fell short of them in the conformation of their bodies. [5] After vanquishing all the neighbouring nations, and learning by report the glory of our ancestors, they assembled the most powerful of their allies, and with high expectations marched against this city. Here they first met with enemies capable to resist them: when matched with our ancestors they appeared in all the natural timidity of their sex, and showed themselves less women in their external appearance than in their weakness and coward-

The Amazons

ice. [6] They had not even the melancholy advantage of making known at home the miscarriage of their own enterprise, and the glory of our exploits. They reaped the full fruits of their folly, and all perished on the spot. Thus did they render the name of this country immortal by the disgrace of their own, and ambitiously attempting to acquire the territory of their neighbours, they lost themselves.

After the expedition of the seven against Thebes

[7] Again, in the expedition against Thebes, after Adrastus and Polynices had fallen in the field, the Thebans would not permit their dead bodies to be buried. Our ancestors, considering that, although those heroes had acted unjustly, they were sufficiently punished by death, but that, by denying them the rites of burial, the spirits of the underworld were deprived of due honour, and the laws of religion materially violated, they immediately dispatched ambassadors to remonstrate with the Thebans, [8] to explain the excess and impropriety of their resentment, to inform them that it belonged to the brave to punish their enemies when alive, but that it was the part of such only as distrusted their own courage, to insult the bodies of the dead. The ambassadors however returned without success; and our ancestors, not prompted by former resentment against the Thebans, not in order to ingratiate themselves with the Argives who were alive, [9] but merely to obtain for

the dead their due and customary honours, bravely taking the field, endangered their own persons for the mutual safety of the contending parties; preventing the Thebans from being impious towards the Gods, and the Argives from being deprived of their paternal rites, the common ceremonies of the Greeks, and the general expectation of all mankind. [10] Governed by these generous principles, and contemning all the dangers of war, while they had justice on their side, they marched forth against a numerous foe, and proved victorious in the field. Their success, however, did not elate them beyond the bounds of moderation: They pushed their advantages no farther than to obtain what they had originally demanded, and they only punished the baseness of the Thebans by contrasting it with their own magnanimity. They got possession of the dead bodies, carried them off the field, and buried them in Eleusis, a borough in their own territory.

[11] Disinterested as this conduct was, the part which they afterwards acted, with regard to the descendants of Hercules, was not less honourable. When that hero had been taken from earth to be numbered with the Gods, his posterity flying from the violence of Eurystheus, wherever they sought refuge, had been successively expelled by the inhabitants, who, though fully sensible of their baseness in doing so, were intimidated by Eurystheus' power, into a compliance with his commands. To these unhappy men, every where pursued and every where abandoned, our ancestors erected an asylum, [12] from which all the promises and threats of their persecutor were unable to ravish them. Their veneration for the character of Hercules, their innate love of justice, prevailed over the expectation of Eurystheus' friendship or the dread of his arms. [13] When all Peloponnesus was assembled under his banner, they did not shrink at the near approach of danger, but con-

The children of Heracles

tinued firm in their resolution. They had received no particular favour from Hercules; they knew his posterity only by their misfortunes; [14] and Eurystheus had never given them occasion of complaint. But they conceived themselves the protectors of innocence, and the scourge of oppression; they thought it the part of liberty to do nothing by compulsion, of justice to assist the injured, and of courage to die, when necessary, in defence of these maxims. [15] It was determined therefore on both sides to come to extremities. Eurystheus disdained receiving the supplicants as a favour from the Athenians, and they determined not to deliver them up even at his entreaty. An engagement must decide whether our ancestors should prevail over the united force of Peloponnesus. Their valour overcame all opposition, they delivered the Heraclides from present and future danger, and crowned the virtues of the father in rewarding his posterity. [16] And in this the children were far more fortunate than the father; that *he*, whose life was one continued course of danger and glory, could never punish Eurystheus, his most inveterate enemy, but *they* saw performed by our ancestors what Hercules could never accomplish, and in one day derived safety to themselves, and took vengeance on their foe.

[17] Such then are the noble occasions on which those, from whom we are defended, displayed their regard to justice, and their valour in maintaining it. The first formation of their society was not like the original establishments of other men. They were not a promiscuous collection of banditti who wished to acquire territory by violence and injustice. The Athenians ever
Autochthony   dwelt in Attica, having the same land for their nurse, their mother, and their native country.

[18] They were the first and only people in those times who, dissolving the petty principalities which the law of the strongest had established, erected an equal

form of government. They regarded the liberty of all as the surest bond of domestic union, and as the best defence against external violence. [19] Wild animals, said they, must be governed by force; men should dread no power but that of the law, and obey no voice but that of reason. [20] With such an origin and such sentiments, they performed the most wonderful exploits, in commemoration of which, their descendants, not despairing of being able to rival their virtue, have erected the most conspicuous monuments.

Unaided they twice exposed their lives for the general safety. [21] The king of Asia, unsatisfied with his present greatness, and actuated by a boundless ambition, prepared an army of five hundred thousand men, hoping by this mighty force to reduce Europe under his subjection. As he knew the superiority of Athens, and that its inhabitants, vanquished by force or gained over by persuasion, would leave the rest of Greece an easy conquest, he made a descent on Marathon; thinking to embarrass and confound our ancestors, if, before they had time to concert measures for repelling the invasion, they should be obliged at once to come to a decisive engagement. [22] He was convinced also, from a knowledge of their character, that though he should direct his attack towards any other state, he would have to contend not only with its inhabitants but also with our ancestors, who, instantly taking the alarm, would generously fly to its assistance; but if he began by invading Attica, the other Greeks, he thought, would not, for the safety of their neighbours, expose themselves to the resentment of so powerful an enemy. [23] Such were the views of the Barbarian; but the Athenians, not yielding to timid suggestions, and regarding a glorious death as the only danger to which they were exposed, dreaded not so much the Persian numbers as they trusted in the Athenian bravery: ashamed to find their country

Equal government under law

ii. Historical period
§§21–66

Accomplishments in the Persian Wars
§§21–47

Darius' attack on Marathon, 490 B.C.

invaded without resistance, they waited not until their allies should come to their relief, or even be made acquainted with their danger, but marching alone against an enemy incomparably more numerous and better prepared, they acquired that safety to the Greeks, for which they had disdained to stand indebted to them. [24] "To die," said they, "is common to all, but to die bravely is peculiar to few. Let us not then regard our lives as what properly belongs to us, but by exposing them for the public cause, let us acquire a renown that shall be peculiar and truly our own. If we cannot conquer alone, neither could we though accompanied by our allies; if we be worsted, our destruction will be only the prelude to theirs; but if we prove victorious, ours will be the glory of defending the liberties of Greece." [25] Their behaviour in the field corresponded to those sentiments. Disregarding their lives, dreading their own laws more than the enemy's sword, and bravely victorious, they erected on the confines of Attica, a monument not more disgraceful to the Persians, or more honourable for themselves, than beneficial to the Grecian name. [26] With such rapidity was this accomplished, that the other states of Greece learned by the same messenger the invasion of the Persians and their defeat, and, without the terror of danger, felt the pleasure of deliverance. It is not surprising then, that such actions, though ancient, should still retain the full verdure of glory, and remain to succeeding ages the examples and envy of mankind.

[27] But many causes conspired to engage Xerxes, king of Asia, to undertake a second expedition against Europe. Disgraced by past misfortunes, irritated by disappointment, and violently incensed against the Greeks, his haughty spirit gave way to the most unbounded schemes of vengeance; and after ten years preparation he landed in Europe with a fleet of twelve hundred sail,

Xerxes' invasion, 480 B.C.

16

and such a number of land-forces, that it would be tedious to recount even the names of those various nations by which he was attended: [28] But what may give some idea of this immense armament is, that though he might have conveyed his troops over Hellespont in twelve hundred ships, he rejected this mode of transporting them, and [29] equally contemning the conceptions of men and the arrangement of the Gods, he made a journey through the sea and a voyage by the land, joining the opposite shores of the Hellespont, and dividing Mount Athos. Every thing yields to the influence of his power or at his artifice. Some are overcome by violence, others restrained by fear, many bribed into subjection. [30] But on this occasion the Athenians were not wanting to themselves or to the general safety. They embarked on board the fleet, and sailed to expect him at Artemisium; while the Lacedaemonians and a few allies, animated with the same spirit, fly to the straights of Thermopylae, and guard the passage into Greece. [31] Both engagements were fought at the same time, but with different success. The Athenians were victorious, but the Lacedaemonians, not deficient in valor, but deceived in the number both of their allies and of the enemy,—they were not conquered,—but perished to a man where they had been drawn up to fight. [32] By this misfortune the Persian became master of Thermopylae; and the Athenians, now reduced to the utmost difficulties, could neither take the field without exposing their city to his fleet, nor embark in their gallies without leaving it at the mercy of his troops. Unable to resist at once the combined attacks of so powerful an armament, and having but this miserable alternative either to forsake Athens, [33] or to unite with the Barbarians in enslaving Greece, they preferred a virtuous liberty with poverty and flight, to servitude with riches and disgrace, and gloriously abandoned their city in

A bridge over the Hellespont and a canal through Mt. Athos

480 B.C.

defence of their country. [34] Having transported their wives and children to Salamis, they there collected the ships of their allies, and patiently waited the arrival of the Persian fleet. Soon after appeared these formidable squadrons, in number so immense, that who would not have trembled at their approach? Yet these our ancestors opposed for the general safety! [35] What were the feelings of those who saw them embark? What did they themselves feel when they considered the prizes laid up in the isle of Salamis? [36] Their destruction, from the infinite superiority of the enemy's numbers, appeared inevitable: but the fate of their wives, and children, was an object of the cruelest anxiety: For what humiliating insults might not these expect to suffer from triumphant Barbarians? [37] Surely, in their present situation the Athenians often embraced, and joined right hands; they probably lamented their condition, when they compared the strength of the Barbarians with their own;—and when no one circumstance could afford them relief. Their city was deserted, their temples burnt or demolished, their country laid waste, and every new form of calamity and disgrace awaited their kindred and themselves. [38] But when they heard the mingled paeans of Greeks and Persians, the exhortations on both sides, the cries of the dying, and saw the sea teeming with the dead, many ships on both sides shattered or sunk, the battle long doubtful, now thinking they were victorious and now that they were overcome, torn between hope and fear, [39] their imaginations presenting many objects they did not see, their minds terrified with sounds they did not hear—how many were their prayers to the Gods? How often did they mention their sacrifices? How great was the pity for their children, the anxiety for their wives? their compassion for their parents? How dreadful were the presages of their future calamities? [40] What God so cruel as not to commiserate them!

Battle of
Salamis,
480 B.C.

18

What mortal so insensible as not to lament them! What heart so base as not to admire their virtue! For surely, by the vigour both of their councils and actions they distinguished themselves above the weakness of humanity; abandoning their city, embarking in gallies, exposing their persons, few in number, against the millions of Asia. [41] Their victory is the fairest monument of liberty, and proves that an handful of freemen contending for their rights, is more powerful than an host of slaves, laboring with infamy to infringe them.

[42] Such were the transactions of the Athenians under Themistocles; a man unmatched in eloquence, council, or action. As their own ships were more numerous than those of all the allies, their sailors more experienced, their soldiers more valiant, and their commanders more distinguished both for bravery and conduct, [43] they carried off, without competition, the palm of victory, and obtained, by universal consent, a distinction proportional to their merit: For their courage appeared to be neither accidental nor spurious, but the genuine produce of their race, and [44] by encountering dangers peculiar to themselves, had diffused advantages over all Greece.

But the inhabitants of Peloponnesus, now thinking themselves secure against naval descents, and forgetting the general interest of their country, began to fortify the isthmus with a view to their particular safety. [45] On this occasion our ancestors acquainted them, that if they continued in that resolution, it would be necessary to throw a wall round all Peloponnesus; because, if provoked by the treachery of their allies, they themselves should unite with the common enemy, the king of Persia would no longer have occasion for a thousand sail to become master of the sea, nor could the fortification of the isthmus alone, much avail the Peloponnesians. [46] Upon this spirited remonstrance the design was laid

Athens
threatens
the Pelo-
ponnesians

aside; and the inhabitants of Peloponnesus, ashamed of
their intentions, became sensible of the danger menaced
by our ancestors, and cheerfully taking the field, atoned
for their past baseness by the glorious victory at Plataea.
Accompanied by the Tegeans alone (for the other allies,
intimidated by the enemy's numbers, had deserted in
the night) the Spartans discomfited and put to flight the
Persians; while the Athenians, assisted by the citizens
of Plataea, chastised such ignoble Greeks as, forgetting
their name and their country, had submitted to a disgraceful servitude. [47] This day only was wanting to
perfect the glory of our ancestors; for now by sea and
land, against Greeks and Barbarians, they gave the
most distinguished proofs of their valour and love of
liberty, and were deemed worthy of being honoured
with the first rank in Greece, as well by those whom they
defeated as by their companions in the victory.

[48] Again, when war broke out among the Greeks
themselves, a war undertaken through envy and fo-
mented by emulation, our ancestors, without foreign
assistance, checked the insolence of Aegina and its con-
federates; and vanquishing their united power in a naval
engagement, carried off seventy gallies. [49] On another occasion, they maintained a war against both
Aegina and Egypt, and while their fleet and army, con-
sisting of all Athenians of military age, were employed
in contending with these formidable enemies, the Corinthians, supported by powerful aid, seized on this favourable opportunity for invading our territories; expecting
that they must either find them altogether defenceless, or
compel the Athenians to withdraw their forces from
Aegina. But they were disappointed in both these views.
[50] The old men and the young, who alone remained in
Athens, trusted to their own bravery for repelling the
invasion. The force of the one had not yet attained its
maturity, that of the other had unhappily begun to de-

Victory at
Plataea,
479 B.C.

Compare
Thucydides
I 105

459 B.C.?

cay; faded or unripe, however, only in their persons, their minds were both blooming and vigorous, [51] the one possessing courage by nature, the other having confirmed it by experience. [52] Nor did they even allow the enemy to enter into the Athenian territories, but marching forth into the neutral country of Megara, with Myronides their general, they prevented their farther progress by obtaining over them a complete victory, as honourable for the victors, as disgraceful to the vanquished. [53] Having erected a trophy in commemoration of it, they returned home; the aged to hold their councils, the young to prosecute their education.

[54] But it is difficult for one speaker to do justice to so extensive a subject, or properly to describe in one day the accumulated glory of ages. For what time, what orator, or what panegyric is sufficient to display the virtue of those who lie interred here? [55] By the most daring and splendid attempts, and with infinite fatigue and danger, they acquired liberty to Greece, and preeminence for Athens. During seventy years, in which they continued masters of the sea, the fruits of their superiority were most conspicuous: No seditions in the Grecian cities; no attempts on the liberty of their allies; [56] no state, I may say no individual, was allowed to domineer over his neighbour, but all were compelled to enjoy equal freedom and independence. They pursued no narrow scheme for augmenting their relative strength, but invigorating the absolute and common strength of Greece, displayed it before the tyrant of Asia, now no longer intoxicated with his plans of ambition, but resigning part of his dominions, and trembling for the remainder. [57] During all this period, no Persian vessel appeared in our seas, no tyrant reigned in Greece, no city was enslaved by the Barbarians. Such was the moderation or respect with which the virtue of the Athenians inspired their neighbours; and so well did their justice

The Athenian Empire

477–circa 407 B.C.

deserve that superiority which their valour had acquired.

[58] Even their misfortunes afford additional evidence of their merit. The loss of the Athenian fleet in the Hellespont, whether through the fault of the commanders, or by fatality of circumstances, was equally felt over all Greece, the general safety of which seemed inseparably connected with the fortune of one state: [59] for, soon after this miscarriage, the command of Greece was committed to other hands, and new leaders were appointed. These were worsted in a sea engagement by an enemy who formerly had been compelled to abandon that element. The Barbarians sail over, without opposition, into Europe; the face of Greece is changed and disfigured; its citizens carried into slavery, or subjected to tyrants at home. [60] It becomes Greece to wear ensigns of mourning, and to pour forth her lamentations at this tomb. Here was her liberty interred with these victims. How unfortunate was she in losing them? How happy was the Persian monarch in having new leaders to contend with? Deprived of such friends, Greece had nothing left but the gloomy prospect of servitude; delivered from such enemies, the monarch of Persia saw his views of ambition open before him, and he was once more elevated with the hopes of executing his father's designs.

[61] Nor, as citizens or as men, must we forget that band of patriots, who, reviving our political constitution at the peril of their lives, re-established the democracy. Not compelled by law, but persuaded by reason, they marched forth into the Piraeus, and maintaining the character of their ancestors, [62] by preferring freedom and death to life and slavery, they rendered the government, then engrossed by a few, a common good in which all the citizens were concerned. The injustice of their adversaries did not more excite their resentment, than their own wretched condition roused their indignation;

Battle of
Aegospotami,
405 B.C.

Sparta's
hegemony

Persian
ascendancy
after battle
of Cnidus,
395 B.C.

Restoration
of democracy
in Athens,
403 B.C.

and, deprived of the first right of humanity, they determined to regain it, or to perish in the attempt. Virtuous oaths and engagements were their only allies; but added to their ancient and inveterate foes, they had their fellow-citizens to contend with. [63] The sepulchres of the Lacedaemonians, still remaining on the spot, are monuments of that victory, by which union and tranquillity were restored to a state, torn by seditions; by which a city, naked and defenceless, was fortified and secured; by which Athens, who had sunk into contempt, reassumed her former rank, and made good her former pretensions.

Spartan garrison troops wounded, 403 B.C.

[64] The same generous principles which had engaged the Athenians to undertake this expedition, still actuated those who survived it. Reinstated in the rank of citizens, their desires were gratified. They did not persecute their enemies with an unrelenting hatred, but determined never to yield to the slavery to which these had basely submitted, they invited them to share the freedom which they themselves had so gloriously acquired.

[65] The success of the present enterprise proves, that it was neither from their own misconduct, nor the valour of their foes, that the past misfortunes of this state had proceeded. If, while divided by factions at home, and surrounded by dangers from abroad, they yet made their way into the bosom of their country, notwithstanding the opposition of the Peloponnesians: How weak must this opposition have proved, had they been united among themselves? [66] But their virtue surely deserved immortal honour, and must excite the emulation of the brave in all succeeding ages.

Neither ought we to forget those strangers who fought in the cause of freedom, thinking virtue their native inheritance, and dying with so much glory, that they were lamented in public, buried at the expense of

Metoics

23

the state, and thought worthy to be afterwards distinguished with honours till then reserved for the citizens.

The accomplishments of those buried today, §§67–76

[67] The Athenians now buried, fell in a similar cause, but still more glorious. They perished for the liberties of those who hated them. They assisted the Corinthians their inveterate foes, when abandoned by their ancient allies, and endangered in their freedom. While the Lacedaemonians envied the prosperity of their friends, these generous Athenians pitied the distress of their enemies, and even died to relieve them. [68] Not regarding their ancient variance with Corinth, or the injuries received from that state, they took the field in order that the Corinthians, instead of being subjected to the yoke of Lacedaemon, might share in the liberties of Athens.

[69] To men actuated by so generous a motive, death was disarmed of all its terrors; dying or living their condition was worthy of envy. Early instructed in the glory of their ancestors, they shewed themselves determined to maintain it; [70] and repairing by their present valour, the effects of past miscarriages, and removing the danger at a distance from their country, they died, as brave ought, leaving trophies to the public, but woes to their kindred. [71] It becomes us then to honour the dead, and to lament the living. For what pleasure, what consolation remains to them? They are deprived of those who loved them, but who, preferring virtue to every connexion, have left them fatherless, widowed, and forlorn. [72] Of all their relatives, the children, too young to feel their loss, are least to be lamented; but most of all, the parents, who are too old ever to forget it. They nourished and brought up children to be the comforts of their age, but of these, in the decline of life, they are deprived, and with them all of their hopes. [73] What can be more miserable? Is not death

24

only to be wished for? Their children, who formerly rendered them the objects of envy, now render them the objects of compassion. The height of their merit, in which they used to glory, now plunges them into deeper distress. [74] What circumstances can put a period to their sorrows?—When the state is unfortunate? Public calamities will be added to private woes—When the state is successful? Others will enjoy the fruits of their children's virtues.—In private dangers? The friends of their prosperity will avoid sharing in their wretchedness; and their enemies, swoln with insolence, will triumph in their misfortunes. [75] We shall best honour the dead then, by extending our protection to the living. We must assist and defend their widows, protect and honour their parents, embrace and cherish their orphans. [76] Who deserve more honour than the dead? Who are entitled to more sympathy than their kindred?

[77] But wherefore this sorrow? Are we ignorant of our common fate? Why bear with impatience what we have ever expected? Why revolt against the law of necessity, since Death is equal to the hero and to the coward, neither overlooking the villain in contempt, nor sparing, in admiration of his character, the man of highest virtue? [78] If those who escape the dangers of war could also escape death, the tide of your sorrows ought ever to flow. But since human nature must yield to age and disease, and the divinity that presides over our fate is inexorable, [79] those are to be reckoned of all men most happy, who, not committing themselves to fortune, or waiting the uncertain approaches of a natural death, choose and embrace that which is most glorious. Dying for whatever is most respectable among men, their memories never fade, their honours ever bloom, their actions remain perpetual objects of emulation and praise, and [80] though lamented as mortal by nature, they are celebrated as immortal through virtue. They

Consolation, §§77–81

are buried at public expense, and contests of strength, wisdom, and magnificence are appointed in honour of them and the gods. [81] For my part, I account them most happy; I envy them their death. Those men alone are gainers by their birth, who, though their bodies be mortal, have acquired immortal renown. But, according to established practice, and the laws of our ancestors, we must mourn for the persons here buried.

From the
PANEGYRICUS OF ISOCRATES

INTRODUCTION

The struggle of Athens, Thebes, and Corinth against Sparta of which Lysias spoke in his *Funeral Oration* came to a sorry end. After some eight years of fighting (395–87 B.C.) Sparta was able to secure diplomatic and military support not only from her old ally Syracuse but also from her old enemy Persia. Antalcidas, the Spartan leader, and Artaxerxes, the Persian king, agreed to the terms of a peace and imposed them on a reluctant Greece. The Greek cities in Cyprus and in what is Turkey today were surrendered to Persian domination while the basis of Thebes' power, her hegemony over the neighboring Boeotian cities, was dissolved. Greece seemed in effect to be ruled by a Persian king and a Spartan viceroy. The settlement was one of Artaxerxes' greatest triumphs; even the Old Testament book of *Esther* bears witness to it:

> And the king Ahasuerus laid a tribute upon the
> land and upon the isles of the sea.
>
> (*Esther* 10. 1)

It was hard for the Greeks to forget that a century before their ancestors had twice turned back invasions of the Persians or that a little over a decade earlier a band of Greek mercenaries, hired by Cyrus and after his death treacherously deprived of their leaders, had cut and plotted their way through an empire too weak to destroy them and too afraid to stop them. The "King's Peace," as the settlement came to be known, was widely regarded as a betrayal

27

of the independence, heritage, and integrity of Greece. To Isocrates (436–338 B.C.) the Peace was not only disgraceful but disastrous, for it encouraged the perpetuation of Greek factionalism, internecine strife and economic stagnation. Around 380 B.C. Isocrates turned his attention to a topic that had been treated long before by that eloquent Sicilian rhetorician, Gorgias of Leontini, and more recently by Lysias, a call for a Panhellenic expedition against Persia. Though in reality a pamphlet intended for a reading public, the appeal for the invasion of the barbarians takes the form of an address to the Greeks assembled for the festival (*panegyris*) of the Olympic games. The *Panegyricus* is an odd blend of contraries. To an unoriginal, although under the circumstances daring, theme Isocrates applied the mythological and rhetorical elaboration expected of any orator but also a new and distinctive stylistic polish for which he was soon to become famous. The exalted, almost chauvinistic, praise of Athens combines with an equally empassioned Panhellenism, just as the idealistic call for Greek cooperation accompanies a clear-sighted perception of the realities of Greek politics and foreign policy. Much of the power of this widely acclaimed speech derives from this very union of opposites. The reader finds himself caught between an increasingly clear and discouraging picture of the present and ever more attractive promises for the future.

Despite this, the proposal for an invasion was not adopted by Isocrates' readers. To them, as to many a modern historian, the idea of the Greeks ever pitting their tenuous unity against the vast continental resources of Persia must have seemed chimerical. It is true that the success which Euagoras of Cyprus had recently had in rallying much of the eastern Mediterranean against Persia (*Panegyricus* § 161) gives some grounds for thinking that Isocrates was not entirely naif in calling for action against Persia, but, as he himself later came to realize, the venture ultimately depended on strong and unified leadership, not from a city-state, but from a powerful individual. Isocrates' proposal thus remained for many years a patient attendant on the

progress of Greek history until, as will appear, it found at last
an unexpected fulfillment.

John Gillies is the translator.

The introduction of Isocrates' speech is devoted to
a justification of his plan to speak on a familiar
theme, the need for an attack on the Persians. He
promises, however, to speak on this traditional
subject in a way that is new and relevant to the
contemporary problems of Athens:

[15] All those who have spoken in this assembly advise you to lay aside your private differences, and to
levy war against the Barbarians. They have enumerated
the unhappy consequences of your civil commotions, and
described the important advantages which might result
from a distant expedition. Their opinion surely is just,
and their arguments in support of it are well founded;
but they place them not in that light which is most
favourable for their cause.

[16] The different states of Greece are divided into
two parties, according to their form of government. At
the head of one are the Lacedaemonians, the other depends entirely on Athens. To think then of making all
these discordant members act harmoniously, without
first adjusting to one design the powers which actuate
and control them, betrays an ignorance both of public
affairs and of the invariable nature of things. [17] If we
intend therefore not merely to make an ostentatious pa-
rade of a vain eloquence, but to benefit you by practical
advice, we must endeavour to reconcile Athens and
Sparta; we must engage these rival states to lay aside
the enmity which divides them, and by their united
force to acquire that superiority over the Barbarians
which at present they are so desirous of usurping over
each other.

[18] It would be easy to bring Athens to this resolution; but the Spartans, naturally inflexible, are confirmed in their present obstinacy by a national prejudice. They believe that by hereditary right they are entitled to the supremacy of Greece. But if it should be proved, that this very title which they allege in their favour is actually against them, and might be claimed by Athens with more propriety and reason, perhaps they may depart from a pretension, not more haughty and unjust than inconsistent with the public interest. [19] From this topic your speakers should have set out; and before enlarging on the principles which we all agree in, they ought to have removed the causes of our dissension.

For my part, there are two reasons which engage me to undertake this task; the first and principal, that you may be throughly reconciled with one another, and persuaded to turn all your resentment against the Barbarians; [20] the second, that, if unsuccessful in this principal design, I may at least have an opportunity of pointing out the obstacles to your happiness, and of proving in the face of this assembly the ancient superiority of Athens on the sea, and its present title to assert the first rank among the Greeks.

> In the next few sections Isocrates iterates the Athenians' claim to be the oldest of the Greek peoples, for they, unlike others who migrated into Greece, were autochthonous. He then turns to the services the Athenians have performed for other Greeks:

[28] To begin with the first and most necessary demand of human nature, you will find that our ancestors were they who supplied it. Though what I am going to relate may be disfigured by tradition or fable, the substance of it is not the less deserving of your regard. When Ceres wandered from one country to another in

quest of her daughter, who had been carried off by violence, she received in Attica the most favourable treatment, and those particular good offices which it is lawful to make known only to the initiated. The goddess was not ungrateful for such favours, but in return, conferred on our ancestors the two most valuable presents which either heaven can bestow, or mankind can receive; the practice of agriculture, which delivered us from the fierce and precarious manner of life common to us with wild animals; and the knowledge of those sacred mysteries which fortify the initiated against all the terrors of death, and inspire them with the pleasing hopes of an happy immortality.

The Eleusinian Mysteries

[29] Our ancestors discovered as much benevolence in dispensing these favours as piety in obtaining them; for their humanity communicated what their virtue had acquired. These mysteries were annually unveiled to all desirous to receive them; and the practice, the means, the advantages of agriculture, were diffused over all Greece.

The following sections recount other services of the Athenians to the Greeks, especially political, economic, and cultural benefits, among them the encouragement of Philosophy and Rhetoric:

[47] Athens also is the seat of philosophy, which hath contrived and established all those institutions which hath softened our manners and regulated our conduct; and which, by teaching us to distinguish between evils brought upon us by imprudence, and those inflicted by necessity, hath enabled us to ward off the one, and to bear the other honourably. [48] Athens likewise is the theatre of eloquence, a talent which all men are ambitious to acquire, and which excites so much envy against those who actually possess it. She has ever been sensible that speech is the original characteristic

Philosophy

Rhetoric

31

of human nature, and that it is by the employment of it alone we acquire all those powers which distinguish us from other animals. She has ever been sensible that fortune might disturb the order of events, confound the designs of the wise, and give success to the rash attempts of folly and inexperience; but that the art of speaking with eloquence and force was superior even to fortune, and could never be acquired but by men of judgment and ability; [49] that eloquence formed the true distinction between the rustic and the sage; that it was neither by their valour, their riches nor any such advantages, but by their eloquence alone, that those who had received a liberal education rendered themselves conspicuous; that this was the surest test of the manner in which each of us had been educated; that it was by eloquence, in fine, we not only acquired an irresistible influence over those among whom we lived, but diffused our reputation and extended our power over countries the most remote from us. [50] In eloquence and philosophy, therefore, Athens so far excels all other nations, that those who are considered as novices at home, become masters elsewhere; that the name of *Greek* is not employed to denote the inhabitant of a particular country, but rather the talents for which the men of that country are distinguished; and that this appellation is more frequently bestowed on such as are acquainted with our literature, than on those who were born in our territories.

"Greek" a cultural, not an ethnic, term

> The next sixty-four sections concern for the most part the wars which Athens waged from times known only through myths up to the end of the Peloponnesian War. In this survey, which is similar in many respects to the summary of Athenian history in Lysias' *Funeral Oration*, Isocrates emphasizes Athens' devotion to Greek freedom and draws a sharp contrast between Athens' glorious

past and the disgraceful conduct of Sparta in more recent times. He then turns to attack the King's Peace of 386 B.C.:

[115] Nor ought we to prefer, to a natural dependence on Athens, that pretended equality and freedom which exists indeed in the treaties and agreements, but which has no foundation among the states of Greece. For who can desire the continuance of such a situation as the present, when pirates command the sea, and ruffians are masters of the land? [116] When the citizens fight within their walls instead of opposing their foreign enemies? When more states are enslaved than before the making of the peace? and when those who still inhabit their native country are more miserable than the exiles? because, on account of the frequency of unhappy revolutions, the former tremble at being involved in those calamities from which the latter hope to be delivered. [117] And so far is Greece from enjoying any degree of the freedom and independence stipulated in that delusive peace, that some cities are subject to tyrants, others are governed by viceroys, while the rest are either torn by faction and sedition, or enslaved by the Persians; those proud invaders, who, in the height of their insolence and power, formerly passed over into Europe, but who found in Athens so vigorous an adversary, [118] that, returning from their expedition with disgrace, they suffered their own territories to be wasted without daring to defend them. They were reduced into such humiliation and distress, they who had crossed our seas with twelve hundred sail, that they durst not bring one ship of war beyond Phaselis; that they were glad, by the most mortifying concessions, to purchase a dishonourable peace, and despairing of any speedy revolution in their favour, waited in anxious and uncertain hopes of ever repairing their misfortunes.

King's Peace, 386 B.C.

Athens' fifth century victories over Persia

The attack on Sparta continues for a while but Isocrates soon turns to criticize all the Greeks for allowing themselves to be divided and dominated by the barbarian king of Persia.

[133] Were any stranger to become a spectator of our ordinary behaviour, I am convinced he would imagine us to be madmen. We contend for trifles amongst ourselves; we waste and destroy our own pitiful possessions; but we neglect the fertile plains of Asia, which lie open to our invasion. [134] The Barbarian knows that nothing is more for his interest than a continuance of our divisions, and therefore he foments them; but we are so far from disturbing the order of his affairs, or from raising seditions among his subjects, that we do not even avail ourselves of the commotions which fortune has stirred up, but, on the contrary, we endeavour to quell them. Of the two armies in Cyprus, we suffer the Persian to employ the one in besieging the other; though both be originally from Greece, [135] and though the island which has revolted from him be well-disposed towards the Athenians, and actually submits itself to the protection of Lacedaemon. The best of his infantry, and the soldiers under Tiribazus, are from Greece; the fleet is manned chiefly by Ionians. All these would with more pleasure be employed in ravaging Asia, than in fighting for small advantages against one another. [136] But we are far from availing ourselves of this disposition of affairs; and, disputing about the Cyclades, these inconsiderable islands, we inadvertently betray to the Barbarian our numerous fleet, and our powerful armies. He is master of these; he threatens those, he lays snares for others; and all of us he equally and with good reason despises. [137] He has at length attained that object at which his predecessors strove in vain to arrive: he is acknowledged king of Persia both by us and by the Lacedaemonians. He is so far master of Greece

Greek mer-
cenaries hired
by Artaxerxes
and Euagoras
of Cyprus

Tension be-
tween Sparta
and Athens

that he demolishes some of her cities, erects fortresses in others; and all this he performs, not by his own power, but through our supine neglect.

To convince his audience that the Persians are not invincible Isocrates now proceeds to show that the barbarians have in the past been able to harm Greece only when Athens and Sparta have not acted in concert. After pointing out a number of past examples of Persian weakness and reminding the Greeks of their traditional hostility to Persia, Isocrates turns to the present state of affairs:

[160] There are many reasons, then, which ought to determine us to march against the Persians; but that which should be the most powerful, is the present conjuncture, for none can be more favourable for such an enterprize. It will be shameful to neglect this opportunity, and to regret it when past. For what situation can we conceive more advantageous than the present for undertaking a Persian war? [161] Have not Egypt and Cyprus revolted from the Great King? Phoenicia and Syria, are they not desolated? Tyre, upon which he had so much dependance, is it not in the hands of his enemies? The greatest part of the cities in Cilicia belong to our friends; the rest may be easily reduced. Lycia never was subject to the Persians. [162] Hecatomnus, governor of Caria, had been long impatient for a revolt; and will join with us whenever we take up arms. That part of Asia which extends from Cnidus to Sinope is inhabited by Greeks, whom it is not necessary to persuade to declare war: they are already so well disposed for this measure, that we have only not to counteract them.

Euagoras of Cyprus desolated Phoenicia and captured Tyre

When Greece is supported by so powerful assistance, and Asia invaded from so many quarters, is it not easy to infer the consequence? Our enemy has been conquered by small divisions of our force; can he ever oppose it when united? [163] The matter then stands thus: if we allow him to strengthen the cities on the coast by augmenting their garrisons, this will speedily bring over to his interest Samos, Rhodes, Chios, and other isles near the continent of Asia: but if we anticipate his designs, and at once render ourselves masters of these cities, it is probable that the inhabitants of Lydia, Phrygia, and even of more distant provinces, intimidated by the neighbourhood of our forces, will think proper to declare themselves in our favour. [164] Let us then make no delay, but avoid, by our present activity, the misfortune which happened to our ancestors. They were too late for the Barbarians; and having abandoned their allies, they, in consequence of this fatal mistake, were obliged to fight against the Persians upon very unequal terms. But if they had pursued the measures to which I now exhort you, if they had been beforehand with their adversary, and had transported the united force of Greece into Asia, they might have conquered the different provinces of that continent successively. [165] For it is evident, that in a war with different countries which lie at a great distance from one another, there should never be time allowed for their assembling their forces together. But our ancestors, paying no attention to this maxim, committed an original error, which nothing but their superior courage could have remedied. If we are wise, we shall avoid their mistake; and taking proper measures from the beginning immediately transport our forces into Lydia and Ionia. [166] We know that the king retains these countries, and indeed all Asia, in an involuntary subjection; ruling them by the terror of his arms, and the number of his troops. If we, therefore, collect an army more powerful than his, which may be done when we please, the inhabitants of Asia will submit without resistance; and we

Athens' withdrawal from the Ionian Revolt, circa 498 B.C.

shall acquire, and peaceably enjoy the possession of all that continent. This is a worthy prize; this is an object more noble than the pre-eminence for which we at present contend.

[167] It is just that the age in which we live should be yet distinguished by some glorious enterprise, that those who have been so long oppressed, may, in some period of their lives, know what it is to be happy. This unfortunate generation has already paid its just tribute to misery. What calamities hath it not suffered? To those inseparably connected with human nature, we have added others still worse. [168] Many citizens have perished unjustly in the bosom of their country: others have been obliged to wander with their wives and children through inhospitable lands: and others, still more wretched, have been compelled by a fatal necessity to carry arms against their friends for those who oppressed them. But these events do not move your compassion; and while you lament the unfortunate heroes of fiction whose history is represented on your theatres, you are so insensible to real calamities, the unhappy consequences of war, and the miserable fruits of your ambition, that you take more delight in the evils which you have inflicted on one another, than even in your own prosperity. [169] I shall be derided perhaps, for pitying the misfortunes of individuals in an age when Italy has been ravaged, Sicily reduced into slavery, many states subjected to the Barbarians, and all the rest of Greece placed in the most imminent danger; [170] yet I cannot help expressing my surprise that those with whom the administration of the public affairs of Greece was entrusted, should neither have foreseen these evils, nor taken proper measures to prevent them. Had they been deserving of the rank which they held, they would have laid aside every other project, and set themselves to advise and exhort us to undertake a distant expedition.

Mercenaries

[171] Perhaps they might have succeeded; if they had not, they would have left their counsels behind them, as honourable testimonies to posterity.

[172] But the leaders of Greece seem to be wholly occupied about lesser objects: They leave to us, who have no share in the government, the care of your more important concerns: The narrower therefore the views of our magistrates, the more extensive ought to be those of the people. Let them by their private wisdom contrive to put an end to our present troubles. The treaties of peace are insufficient for their purpose: they may retard, but cannot prevent our misfortunes; and whenever we find a favourable occasion of committing any signal injury against one another, we shall be ready still to embrace it. [173] But we stand in need of some more durable plan of accommodation, which will forever put an end to our hostilities, and unite us by the lasting ties of mutual affection and fidelity. The method I propose is both simple in theory and easy of execution. Never can there be a lasting peace established among the Greeks until they agree in making war against the Barbarians. It is then, that, animated by the same hopes, excited by common fears, having their resentment directed against the same object, they will be cemented by the most indissoluble attachment. [174] It is then, that the great cause of our animosity will be removed,—that miserable indigence, which destroys every sentiment of nature or of friendship, which engenders strife, which kindles war, which inflames sedition;—and it is then, that, no longer containing the seeds of dissolution, or decay, our union will be as lasting as sincere. Let us determine, therefore, at length, to carry the war into Asia, and to draw this one benefit, at least, from our domestic dissensions, that we shall make use of the experience acquired in them, in fighting against the Barbarians.

38

The final fifteen sections of the speech advance a
few further arguments that the expedition against
Persia is both just and practical and remind the
audience of the advantages to be obtained by
such a venture.

THE FIRST PHILIPPIC OF DEMOSTHENES

INTRODUCTION

Demosthenes was perhaps four years old when Isocrates published his *Panegyricus*. Now, about thirty years later, with his weakness in delivery only recently mastered and carefully warding off any animosity that might be directed against a man so young discussing a subject so difficult, he rises in the assembly to deliver one of his boldest and most challenging speeches. The subject was one that no one could reasonably have anticipated in the 380's—how to stop the recent advance of the long inactive kingdom of Macedon into areas that Athens considered her proper sphere of interest. In 359 B.C. Philip had become ruler of Macedon. Within a few years he had secured his at first tenuous hold on the throne, bought, then driven off foreign invaders, and mustered a professional army of unparalleled discipline and strength. His determination to consolidate and strengthen his kingdom naturally led him to the lands adjoining his realm—to Chalcidice and Thrace, and the gulf into which the gold-rich river Strymon poured its coveted waters. There in 357 Philip and Athens began their history of conflict. The issue was the control of the town of Amphipolis, which Athens had colonized some eighty years earlier as part of her effort to control the trade routes and gold and timber supply of northern Greece. Amphipolis had long been independent of Athens, but, threatened by the advance of Macedon, turned to the mother city for help. The sorry record of intrigue and duplicity that followed is mercifully obscure, even to this day, but in the end Philip emerged with Amphipolis and an income of a thousand talents a year, more than ten times the amount Demosthenes proposes to raise in section 28 of this speech. In short order by taking Potidaea, Pydna, and

Methone Philip replaced Athenian with Macedonian control of the Thermaic gulf.

Affairs closer to home, troubles in the naval alliance she had developed in the early fourth century, and an optimistic lethargy kept Athens from taking any severe measures against Philip, though she did prevent him from passing the strategic pass at Thermopylae when in 353 B.C. he lead a force into north central Greece. But in 351 B.C. when it was heard that Philip was moving eastward through Thrace ever closer to what Athens knew was a vital part of her grain supply route, the Hellespont, Demosthenes rose to denounce Philip and to propose that Athens expand and reorganize her military force to stop Macedon. The Athenians, convinced alternately that Philip was as invincible as a god and as weak as a dying invalid, did not adopt his suggestions. But Demosthenes had at least caught their attention and in the next few years spoke with increasing frequency and fervor until he could convince Athens that his view of Philip was correct and eventually lead her into a direct confrontation with Macedon.

The translations of Demosthenes used in this volume are by A. W. Pickard-Cambridge, a distinguished Hellenist at Balliol College, Oxford.

---

[1] If some new subject were being brought before us, men of Athens, I would have waited until most of your ordinary advisers had declared their opinion; and if anything that they said were satisfactory to me, I would have remained silent, and only if it were not so, would I have attempted to express my own view. But since we find ourselves once more considering a question upon which they have often spoken, I think I may reasonably be pardoned for rising first of all. For if their advice to you in the past had been what it ought to have been, you would have had no occasion for the present debate.

[2] In the first place, then, men of Athens, we must

Prologue

41

not be downhearted at our present situation, however wretched it may seem to be. For in the worst feature of the past lies our best hope for the future—in the fact, that is, that we are in our present plight because you are not doing your duty in any respect; for if you were doing all that you should do, and we were still in this evil case, we could not then even hope for any improvement. [3] In the second place, you must bear in mind (what some of you have heard from others, and those who know can recollect for themselves), how powerful the Spartans were, not long ago, and yet how noble and patriotic your own conduct was, when instead of doing anything unworthy of your country you faced the war with Sparta in defence of the right. Now why do I remind you of these things? It is because, men of Athens, I wish you to see and to realize, that so long as you are on your guard you have nothing to fear; but that if you are indifferent, nothing can be as you would wish: for this is exemplified for you both by the power of Sparta in those days, to which you rose superior because you gave your minds to your affairs; and by the insolence of Philip today, which troubles us because we care nothing for the things which should concern us. [4] If, however, any of you, men of Athens, when he considers the immense force now at Philip's command, and the city's loss of all her strongholds, thinks that Philip is a foe hard to conquer, I ask him (right though he is in his belief) to reflect also that there was a time when we possessed Pydna and Poteidaea and Methone; when all the surrounding country was our own, and many of the tribes which are now on his side were free and independent, and more inclined to be friendly to us than to him. [5] Now if in those days Philip had made up his mind that it was a hard thing to fight against the Athenians, with all their fortified outposts on his own frontiers, while he was destitute of allies, he would have achieved none of his recent successes, nor acquired this great power. But Philip saw quite clearly, men of Athens, that all these strongholds were prizes of war, displayed for competition. He saw that in the nature of things the property of the absent belongs to those who are on the spot, and that of the negligent to those who are ready for toil and danger. [6] It is, as you know, by acting upon this belief, that he has brought all those places under his power, and now holds them—some of them by right of capture in war, others in virtue of alliances and friendly understandings; for everyone is willing to grant alliance and to give attention to those whom they see to be prepared and ready to take action as is necessary. [7] If then, men of Athens, you also will resolve to adopt this principle to-day—the principle which you have never observed before—if each of you can henceforward be relied upon to throw aside all this pretence of incapacity, and to act where his duty bids him, and where his services can be of use to his country; if he who has money will contribute, and he who is of military age will join the campaign; if, in one plain word, you will resolve henceforth to depend absolutely on yourselves, each man no longer hoping that he will need to do nothing himself, and that his neighbour will do everything for him; then, God willing, you will recover your own; you will take back all that your indolence has lost, and you will have your revenge upon Philip. [8] Do not imagine that his fortune is built to last forever, as if he were a God. He also has those who hate him and fear him, men of Athens, and envy him too, even among those who now seem to be his closest friends. All the feelings that exist in any other body of men must be supposed to exist in Philip's supporters. Now, however, all such feelings are cowed before him; your slothful apathy has taken away their only rallying point; and it is this apathy that I bid you put off to-day. [9] Mark

Philip is
no god

the situation, men of Athens: mark the pitch which the man's outrageous insolence has reached, when he does not even give you a choice between action and inaction, but threatens you, and utters (as we are told) haughty language: for he is not the man to rest content in possession of his conquests: he is always casting his net wider; and while we procrastinate and sit idle, he is setting his toils around us on every side. [10] When, then, men of Athens, when, I say, will you take the action that is required? What are you waiting for? 'We are waiting,' you say, 'till it is necessary.' But what must we think of all that is happening at this present time? Surely the strongest necessity that a free people can experience is the shame which they must feel at their position! What? Do you want to go round asking one another, 'Is there any news?' Could there be any stranger news than that a man of Macedonia is defeating Athenians in war, and ordering the affairs of the Hellenes? [11] 'Is Philip dead?' 'No, but he is sick.' And what difference does it make to you? For if anything should happen to him, you will soon raise up for yourselves a second Philip, if it is thus that you attend to your interests. Indeed, Philip himself has not risen to this excessive height through his own strength, so much as through our neglect. I go even further. [12] If anything happened to Philip—if the operation of Fortune, who always cares for us better than we care for ourselves, were to effect this too for us—you know that if you were at hand, you could descend upon the general confusion and order everything as you wished; but in your present condition, even if circumstances offered you Amphipolis, you could not take it; for your forces and your minds alike are far away.

[13] Well, I say no more of the obligation which rests upon you all to be willing and ready to do your duty; I will assume that you are resolved and convinced.

Demosthenes' proposals

44

But the nature of the armament which, I believe, will set you free from such troubles as these, the numbers of the force, the source from which we must obtain funds, and the best and quickest way, as it seems to me, of making all further preparations—all this, men of Athens, I will at once endeavour to explain when I have made one request of you. [14] Give your verdict on my proposal when you have heard the whole of it; do not prejudge it before I have done; and if at first the force which I propose appears unprecedented, do not think that I am merely creating delays. It is not those whose cry is 'At once,' 'To-day,' whose proposals will meet our need; for what has already happened cannot be prevented by any expedition now. [15] It is rather he who can show the nature, the magnitude, and the financial possibility of a force which when provided will be able to continue in existence either until we are persuaded to break off the war, or until we have overcome the enemy; for thus only can we escape further calamity for the future. These things I believe I can show, though I would not stand in the way of any other speaker's professions. It is no less a promise than this that I make; the event will soon test its fulfilment, and you will be the judges of it.

[16] First then, men of Athens, I say that fifty warships must at once be got in readiness: and next, that you must be in such a frame of mind that, if any need arises, you will embark in person and sail. In addition, you must prepare transports for half our cavalry, and a sufficient number of boats. [17] These, I think, should be in readiness to meet those sudden sallies of his from his own country against Thermopylae, the Chersonese, Olynthus, and any other place which he may select. For we must make him realize that there is a possibility of your rousing yourselves out of your excessive indifference, just as when once you went to Euboea, and before that (as we are told) to Haliartus, and finally,

i. Ships

358 B.C.
395 B.C.

only the other day, to Thermopylae. [18] Such a possibility, even if you are unlikely to make it a reality, as I think you ought to do, is not one which he can treat lightly; and you may thus secure one of two objects. On the one hand, he may know that you are on the alert—he will in fact know it well enough: there are only too many persons, I assure you, in Athens itself, who report to him all that happens here: and in that case his apprehensions will ensure his inactivity. But if, on the other hand, he neglects the warning, he may be taken off his guard; for there will be nothing to hinder you from sailing to his country, if he gives you the opportunity. [19] These are the measures upon which I say you should all be resolved, and your preparations for them made. But before this, men of Athens, you

ii. A standing army

must make ready a force which will fight without intermission, and do him damage. Do not speak to me of ten thousand or twenty thousand mercenaries. I will have none of your paper-armies. Give me an army which will be the army of Athens, and will obey and follow the general whom you elect, be there one general or more, be he one particular individual, or be he who he may. You must also provide maintenance for this force. [20] Now what is this force to be? how large is it to be? how is it to be maintained? how will it consent to act in this manner? I will answer these questions point by point. The number of mercenaries—but you must not repeat the mistake which has so often injured you, the mistake of, first, thinking any measures inadequate, and so voting for the largest proposal, and then, when the time for action comes, not even executing the smaller one; you must rather carry out and make provision for the smaller measure, and add to it, if it proves too small—[21] the total number of soldiers, I say, must be two thousand, and of these five hundred must be Athenians, beginning from whatever age you think good: they must serve for a definite period—not a long one, but one to be fixed at your discretion—and in relays. The rest must be mercenaries. With these must be cavalry, two hundred in number, of whom at least fifty must be Athenians, as with the infantry; and the conditions of service must be the same. You must also find transports for these. [22] And what next? Ten swift ships of war. For as he has a fleet, we need swift-sailing warships too, to secure the safe passage of the army. And how is maintenance to be provided for these? This also I will state and demonstrate, as soon as I have given you my reasons for thinking that a force of this size is sufficient, and for insisting that those who serve in it shall be citizens.

[23] The size of the force, men of Athens, is determined by the fact that we cannot at present provide an army capable of meeting Philip in the open field; we must make plundering forays, and our warfare must at first be of a predatory nature. Consequently the force must not be over-big—we could then neither pay nor feed it—any more than it must be wholly insignificant. [24] The presence of citizens in the force that sails I require for the following reasons. I am told that Athens once maintained a mercenary force in Corinth, under the command of Polystratus, Iphicrates, Chabrias and others, and that you yourselves joined in the campaign with them; and I remember hearing that these mercenaries, when they took the field with you, and you with them, were victorious over the Spartans. But ever since your mercenary forces have gone to war alone, it is your friends and allies that they conquer, while your enemies have grown more powerful than they should be. After a casual glance at the war to which Athens has sent them, they sail off to Artabazus, or anywhere rather than to the war; and the general follows them naturally enough, for his power over them is gone when he can

25 percent of the force to be citizens

391 B.C.

The dangers in using mercenaries

give them no pay. [25] You ask what I bid you do. I bid you take away their excuses both from the general and the soldiers, by supplying pay and placing citizen-soldiers at their side as spectators of these mysteries of generalship; for our present methods are a mere mockery. Imagine the question to be put to you, men of Athens, whether you are at peace or no. 'At peace?' you would say; 'Of course not! We are at war with Philip.' [26] Now have you not all along been electing from among your own countrymen ten captains and generals, and cavalry-officers, and two masters-of-the-horse? and what are they doing? Except the one single individual whom you happen to send to the seat of war, they are all marshalling your processions for you with the commissioners of festivals. You are no better than men modelling puppets of clay. Your captains and your cavalry-officers are elected to be displayed in the streets, not to be sent to the war. [27] Surely, men of Athens, your captains should be elected from among yourselves, and your master-of-the-horse from among yourselves; your officers should be your own countrymen, if the force is to be really the army of Athens. As it is, the master-of-the-horse who is one of yourselves has to sail to Lemnos; while the master-of-the-horse with the army that is fighting to defend the possessions of Athens is Menelaus. I do not wish to disparage that gentleman; but whoever holds that office ought to have been elected by you.

Cost of
proposal ii

[28] Perhaps, however, while agreeing with all that I have said, you are mainly anxious to hear my financial proposals, which will tell you the amount and the sources of the funds required. I proceed, therefore, with these at once. First for the sum. The cost of the bare rations for the crews, with such a force, will be 90 talents and a little over—40 talents for ten swift ships, and 20 minae a month for each ship; and for the soldiers

Over 90 talents a year

48

as much again, each soldier to receive rations to the value of 10 drachmae a month; and for the cavalry (two hundred in number, each to receive 30 drachmae a month) twelve talents. [29] It may be said that the supply of bare rations to the members of the force is an insufficient initial provision; but this is a mistake. I am quite certain that, given so much, the army will provide everything else for itself from the proceeds of war, without injury to a single Hellene or ally of ours, and that the full pay will be made up by these means. I am ready to sail as a volunteer and to suffer the worst, if my words are untrue. The next question then is of ways and means, in so far as the funds are to come from yourselves. I will explain this at once.

[*A schedule of ways and means is read.*]

[30] This, men of Athens, is what we have been able to devise; and when you put our proposals to the vote, you will pass them, if you approve of them; that so your war with Philip may be a war, not of resolutions and dispatches, but of actions.

[31] I believe that the value of your deliberations about the war and the armament as a whole would be greatly enhanced, if you were to bear in mind the situation of the country against which you are fighting, remembering that most of Philip's plans are successfully carried out because he takes advantage of winds and seasons; for he waits for the Etesian winds or the winter-season, and only attacks when it would be impossible for us to effect a passage to the scene of action. [32] Bearing this in mind, we must not carry on the war by means of isolated expeditions; we shall always be too late. We must have a permanent force and armament. As our winter-stations for the army we have Lemnos, Thasos, Sciathos, and the islands in that re-

Defence of
the proposals

The seasonal
north winds

49

gion, which have harbours and corn, and are well supplied with all that an army needs. And as to the time of year, whenever it is easy to approach the shore and the winds are not dangerous, our force can without difficulty lie close to the Macedonian coast itself, and block the mouths of the ports.

[33] How and when he will employ the force is a matter to be determined, when the time comes, by the commander whom you put in control of it. What must be provided from Athens is described in the scheme which I have drafted. If, men of Athens, you first supply the sum I have mentioned, and then, after making ready the rest of the armament—soldiers, ships, cavalry—bind the whole force in its entirety, by law, to remain at the seat of war; if you become your own paymasters, your own commissioners of supply, but require your general to account for the actual operations; then there will be an end of these perpetual discussions of one and the same theme, which end in nothing but discussion: [34] and in addition to this, men of Athens, you will, in the first place, deprive him of his chief source of supply. For what is this? Why, he carries on the war at the cost of your own allies, harrying and plundering those who sail the seas! And what will you gain besides this? You will place yourselves out of reach of disaster. It will not be as it was in the past, when he descended upon Lemnos and Imbros, and went off, with your fellow-citizens as his prisoners of war, or when he seized the vessels off Geraestus, and levied an enormous sum from them; or when (last of all) he landed at Marathon, seized the sacred trireme, and carried it off from the country; while all the time you can neither prevent these aggressions, nor yet send an expedition which will arrive when you intend it to arrive. [35] But for what reason do you think, men of Athens, do the festival of the Panathenaea and the festival of the Dionysia always

Southern tip
of Euboea

take place at the proper time, whether those to whom the charge of either festival is allotted are specially qualified persons or not—festivals upon which you spend larger sums of money than upon any armament whatsoever, and which involve an amount of trouble and preparation, which are unique, so far as I know, in the whole world—; and yet your armaments are always behind the time—at Methone, at Pagasae, at Potidaea? [36] It is because for the festivals all is arranged by law. Each of you knows long beforehand who is to supply the chorus, and who is to be steward of the games, for his tribe: he knows what he is to receive, and when, and from whom, and what he is to do with it. No detail is here neglected, nothing is left indefinite. But in all that concerns war and our preparation for it, there is no organization, no revision, no definiteness. Consequently it is not until the news comes that we appoint our trierarchs and institute exchanges of property for them, and inquire into ways and means. When that is done, we first resolve that the resident aliens and the independent freedmen shall go on board; then we change our minds and say that citizens shall embark; then that we will send substitutes; [37] and while all these delays are occurring, the object of the expedition is already lost. For we spend on preparation the time when we should be acting, and the opportunities which events afford will not wait for our slothful evasions; while as for the forces on which we think we can rely in the meantime, when the critical moment comes, they are tried and found wanting. And Philip's insolence has reached such a pitch, that he has sent such a letter as the following to the Euboeans.

356–52 B.C.

[*The letter is read.*]

[38] The greater part of the statements that have been read are true, men of Athens; and they ought not

to be true! but I admit that they may possibly be unpleasant to hear; and if the course of future events would pass over all that a speaker passes over in his speech, to avoid giving pain, we should be right in speaking with a view to your pleasure. But if attractive words, spoken out of season, bring their punishment in actual reality, then it is disgraceful to blind our eyes to the truth, to put off everything that is unpleasant, [39] to refuse to understand even so much as this, that those who conduct war rightly must not follow in the wake of events, but must be beforehand with them: for just as a general may be expected to lead his army, so those who debate must lead the course of affairs, in order that what they resolve upon may be done, and that they may not be forced to follow at the heels of events. [40] You, men of Athens, have the greatest power in the world—warships, infantry, cavalry, revenue. But none of these elements of power have you used as you ought, down to this very day. The method of your warfare with Philip is just that of barbarians in a boxing-match. Hit one of them, and he hugs the place; hit him on the other side, and there go his hands; but as for guarding, or looking his opponent in the face, he neither can nor will do it. It is the same with you. [41] If you hear that Philip is in the Chersonese, you resolve to make an expedition there; if he is at Thermopylae, you send one there; and wherever else he may be, you run up and down in his steps. It is he that leads your forces. You have never of yourselves come to any salutary decision in regard to the war. No single event do you ever discern before it occurs—before you have heard that something has happened or is happening. Perhaps there was room for this backwardness until now; but now we are at the very crisis, and such an attitude is possible no longer. [42] Surely, men of Athens, it is one of the gods—one who blushes for Athens, as he sees the course which events

A barbarian
prize fighter

are taking—that has inspired Philip with this restless
activity. If he were content to remain at peace, in possession of all that he has won by conquest or by fore-
stalling us—if he had no further plans—even then, the
record against us as a people, a record of shame and
cowardice and all that is most dishonourable, would, I
think, seem complete enough to some of you. But now
he is always making some new attempt, always grasping
after something more; and unless your spirit has utterly
departed, his conduct will perhaps bring you out into
the field. [43] It amazes me, men of Athens, that not one
of you remembers with any indignation, that this war
had its origin in our intention to punish Philip; and that
now, at the end of it, the question is, how we are to
escape disaster at his hands. But that he will not stay
his progress until some one arrests it is plain enough. Are
we then to wait for that? Do you think that all is right,
when you dispatch nothing but empty ships and some-
body's hopes? [44] Shall we not embark? Shall we not
now, if never before, go forth ourselves, and provide at
least some small proportion of Athenian soldiers? Shall
we not sail to the enemy's country? But I heard the
question, 'At what point on his coast are we to anchor?'
The war itself, men of Athens, if you take it in hand, will
discover his weak points: but if we sit at home listening
to the mutual abuse and recriminations of our orators,
you can never realize any of the results that you ought
to realize. [45] I believe that whenever any portion of
Athens is sent with the forces, even if the whole city
does not go, the favour of Heaven and of Fortune fights
on our side. But whenever you dispatch anywhere a
general with an empty resolution and some platform-
hopes to support him, then you achieve nothing that you
ought to achieve, your enemies laugh at you, and your
allies are in deadly fear of all such armaments. [46] It is
impossible, utterly impossible, that any one man should

The poli-
ticians

53

be able to effect all that you wish for you. He can give
undertakings and promises; he can accuse this man and
that; and the result is that your fortunes are ruined. For
when the general is at the head of wretched, unpaid
mercenaries, and when there are those in Athens who
lie to you light-heartedly about all that he does, and,
on the strength of the tales that you hear, you pass decrees at random, what *must* you expect?

[47] How then can this state of things be termi-
nated? Only, men of Athens, when you expressly make
the same men soldiers, witnesses of their general's
actions, and judges at his examination when they return
home; for then the issue of your fortunes will not be a
tale which you hear, but a thing which you will be on
the spot to see. So shameful is the pass which matters
have now reached, that each of your generals is tried
for his life before you two or three times, but does not
dare to fight in mortal combat with the enemy even
once. They prefer the death of kidnappers and brigands
to that of a general. For it is a felon's death, to die by
sentence of the court: the death of a general is to fall
in battle with the enemy. [48] Some of us go about saying
that Philip is negotiating with Sparta for the overthrow
of the Thebans and the breaking up of the free states;
others, that he has sent ambassadors to the king; others,
that he is fortifying cities in Illyria. [49] We all go about
inventing each his own tale. I quite believe, men of
Athens, that he is intoxicated with the greatness of his
successes, and entertains many such visions in his mind;
for he sees that there are none to hinder him, and he is
elated at his achievements. But I do not believe that he
had chosen to act in such a way that the most foolish
persons in Athens can know what he intends to do; for
no persons are so foolish as newsmongers. [50] But if we
dismiss all such tales, and attend only to the certainty—
that the man is our enemy, that he is robbing us of our

Artaxerxes
III, king of
Persia

54

own, that he has insulted us for a long time, that all that we ever expected any one to do for us has proved to be against us, that the future is in our own hands, that if we will not fight him now in his own country we shall perhaps be obliged to do so in ours—if, I say, we are assured of this, then we shall have made up our minds aright, and shall be quit of idle words. For you have not to speculate what the future may be: you have only to be assured that the future must be evil, unless you give heed and are ready to do your duty.

[51] Well, I have never yet chosen to gratify you by saying anything which I have not felt certain would be for your good; and to-day I have spoken freely and without concealment, just what I believe. I could wish to be as sure of the good that a speaker will gain by giving you the best advice as of that which you will gain by listening to him. I should then have been far happier than I am. As it is, I do not know what will happen to me, for what I have said: but I have chosen to speak in the sure conviction that if you carry out my proposals, it will be for your good; and may the victory rest with that policy which will be for the good of all!

Conclusion

THE SECOND OLYNTHIAC
OF DEMOSTHENES

Demosthenes' *First Philippic* was an unquestionably serious and thoughtful contribution to Athenian political discussion, based on careful observation and proposing measures that were at least a partial answer to the problems of Athens as Demosthenes saw them. Whatever one thinks of the wisdom of its policy or the youthful confidence of its author, it is the work of a statesman. The *Second Olynthiac,* delivered two years later in 349 B.C. reveals an important change in the tenor of Athenian political life and in the nature of Demosthenes' oratory. Philip's expansion into Chalcidice in 349 B.C. again brought him into an area that Athens had come to feel belonged in her sphere of influence. Olynthus, the chief city of Chalcidice which was badly worried by the encroachments of Philip, appealed to Athens for alliance. Once again Athens was forced to consider the question of her relations with Philip. Demosthenes' position was predictable. Naturally he opposed Macedon and in three empassioned speeches, much like the *Philippics,* but named *Olynthiacs,* he called for alliance and military support for Olynthus. The response surprised no one, but its tone was new. The studied thoughtfulness of the *First Philippic* is all but gone and a fiery invective has replaced it. The voice with which he speaks is no longer that of a statesman, but of a politician.

Although the speech is of interest for the glimpses it provides into Athenian political organization (§§ 29 and 30) and into the mysterious "secret understanding" between Athens and Philip (§ 6), the opportunity it provides for seeing another side of Demosthenes gives this oration its exceptional value. To a modern reader much of the rhetoric in the following pages may seem strangely familiar. Demosthenes' comments are much like those frequently heard in contemporary political oratory, and reveal some of the most unfortunate and recurring illusions of commentators on foreign policy. He is simultaneously obsessed with the menace of Philip (§ 1) and convinced of his weakness (§ § 14-21). He is sure that the citizenry of Macedon is unhappy and hints that they might even be willing to overthrow their king (§ 15). In a benign trust, he believes stray and un-evaluated sources (§ 17) as long as the information offered conforms to his own notions. At length his characterization of Macedon passes from exaggeration and simple misunderstanding into a melodramatic phantasia of a debauched monarch surrounded by lewd brigands and flatterers (§ § 18 and 19). Then, since he is unwilling to admit that Philip's undeniable strength is due to his popular and capable leadership of a united and enthusiastic kingdom, he must search for other explanations to account for his apparent success. Demosthenes finds the scapegoat he needs in the past mistakes of Athenian policy, and by implication in the leaders responsible for those policies. The foreign problems of Athens come thus to be viewed as external manifestations of her internal politics.

Paradoxically Demosthenes both underestimates and overestimates Philip's power. For all his concentration on the danger and menace of Macedon, he never sees it as a power in its own right, with its own sources of strength and its own national objectives. This attitude of Demosthenes accounts for much in his oratory: his patriotism, his intense "Athenianism," and also for his reluctance to negotiate or to seek a compromise with what he regarded as a transitory and insubstantial (§ 14) phenomenon. No one will deny the skill with which Demosthenes rouses to action a complacent and uncertain people, playing on their pride, their sense of history, their chauvinism, answering their fears and allaying their worries, but the policies and attitudes of the speech are a sad, ancient, and familiar story.

[1] Many as are the occasions, men of Athens, on which we may discern the manifestation of the goodwill of Heaven towards this city, one of the most striking is to be seen in the circumstances of the present time. For that men should have been found to carry on war against Philip; men whose territory borders on his and who possess some power; men, above all, whose sentiments in regard to the war are such that they think of the proposed compact with him, not only as untrustworthy, but as the very ruin of their country—this seems to be certainly the work of a superhuman, a divine, beneficence. [2] And so, men of Athens, we must take care that we do not treat ourselves less well than circumstances have treated us. For it is a shameful thing—nay, it is the very depth of shame—to throw away openly, not only cities and places which were once in our power, but even the allies and the opportunities which have been provided for us by Fortune.

[3] Now to describe at length the power of Philip, men of Athens, and to incite you to the performance of your duty by such a recital, is not, I think, a satisfactory proceeding; and for this reason—that while all that can be said on this subject tends to Philip's glory, it is a story of failure on our part. For the greater the extent to which his success surpasses his deserts, the greater is the admiration with which the world regards him; while, for your part, the more you have fallen short of the right use of your opportunities, the greater is the disgrace that you have incurred. [4] I will therefore pass over such considerations. For any honest inquirer must see that the causes of Philip's rise to greatness lie in Athens, and not in himself. Of the services for which he has to thank those whose policy is determined by his interest—services for which you ought to require their

punishment—the present is not, I see, the moment to speak. But apart from these, there are things which may be said, and which it is better that you should all have heard—things which (if you will examine them aright) constitute a grave reproach against him; and these I will try to tell you.

[5] If I called him perjured and faithless, without giving his actions in evidence, my words would be treated as idle abuse, and rightly: and it happens that to review all his actions up to the present time, and to prove the charge in every case, requires only a short speech. It is well, I think, that the story should be told, for it will serve two purposes; first, to make plain the real badness of the man's character; and secondly, to let those who are over-alarmed at Philip, as if he were invincible, see that he has come to the end of all those forms of deceit by which he rose to greatness, and that his career is already drawing to its close. [6] For I, too, men of Athens, should be regarding Philip with intense fear and admiration, if I saw that his rise was the result of a righteous policy. But when I study and consider the facts, I find that originally, when certain persons wished to drive from your presence the Olynthians who desired to address you from this place, Philip won over our innocent minds by saying that he would deliver up Amphipolis to us, and by inventing the famous secret understanding; [7] that he afterwards conciliated the Olynthians by seizing Potidaea, which was yours, and injuring their former allies by handing it over to themselves; and that, last of all, he recently won over the Thessalians, by promising to give up Magnesia to them, and undertaking to carry on the war with the Phocians on their behalf. There is absolutely no one who has ever had dealings with him that he has not deluded; and it is by deceiving and winning over, one after another, those who in their blindness did not realize what he was, that

Narrative
§§ 5–8

359–57 B.C.
Philip prom-
ises to yield
Amphipolis
to Athens

353 B.C.

he has risen as he has done. [8] And therefore, just as it was by these deceptions that he rose to greatness, in the days when each people fancied that he intended to do some service to themselves; so it is these same deceptions which should drag him down again, now that he stands convicted of acting for his own ends throughout. Such, then, is the crisis, men of Athens, to which Philip's fortunes have now come. If it is not so, let any one come forward and show me (or rather you) that what I say is untrue; or that those who have been deceived at the outset trust him as regards the future; or that those who have been brought into unmerited bondage would not gladly be free.

Anticipation of objections, §§9 and 10

[9] But if any of you, while agreeing with me so far, still fancies that Philip will maintain his hold by force, because he has already occupied fortified posts and harbours and similar positions, he is mistaken. When power is cemented by goodwill, and the interest of all who join in a war is the same, then men are willing to share the labour, to endure the misfortunes, and to stand fast. But when a man has become strong, as Philip has done, by a grasping and wicked policy, the first excuse, the least stumble, throws him from his seat and dissolves the alliance. [10] It is impossible, men of Athens, utterly impossible, to acquire power that will last, by unrighteousness, by perjury, and by falsehood. Such power holds out for a moment, or for a brief hour; it blossoms brightly, perhaps, with fair hopes; but time detects the fraud, and the flower falls withered about its stem. In a house or a ship, or any other structure, it is the foundations that must be strongest; and no less, I believe, must the principles, which are the foundation of men's actions, be those of truth and righteousness. Such qualities are not to be seen to-day in the past acts of Philip.

The proposal §§11–13

[11] I say, then, that we should help the Olynthians; and the best and quickest method which can be proposed

is the method which I approve. Further, we should send an embassy to the Thessalians—to some, to inform them of our intention; to others, to spur them on; for even now they have resolved to demand the restitution of Pagasae, and to make representations in regard to Magnesia. [12] Take care, however, men of Athens, that our envoys may not only have words to speak, but also actions of yours to point to. Let it be seen that you have gone forth in a manner that is worthy of Athens, and are already in action. Words without the reality must always appear a vain and empty thing, and above all when they come from Athens; for the more we seem to excel in the glib use of such language, the more it is distrusted by every one. [13] The change, then, which is pointed out to them must be great, the conversion striking. They must see you paying your contributions, marching to war, doing everything with a will, if any of them is to listen to you. And if you resolve to accomplish all this in very deed, as it should be accomplished, not only will the feeble and untrustworthy nature of Philip's alliances be seen, but the weakness of his own empire and power will also be detected.

[14] The power and the empire of Macedonia is, indeed, to speak generally, an element which tells considerably as an addition to any other power. You found it so when it helped you against the Olynthians in the days of Timotheus; the Olynthians in their turn found its help of some value, in combination with their own strength, against Potidaea; and it has recently come to the aid of the Thessalians, in their disordered and disturbed condition, against the ruling dynasty: and wherever even a small addition is made to a force, it helps in every way. [15] But in itself the Macedonian Empire is weak and full of manifold evils. Philip has in fact rendered his own tenure of it even more precarious than it naturally was, by these very wars and campaigns

Proofs
§§14–30
i. §§14–21
Internal
weaknesses
364–62 B.C.

352 B.C.

61

which might be supposed to prove his power. For you must not imagine, men of Athens, that Philip and his subjects delight in the same things. Philip has a passion for glory—that is his ambition; and he has deliberately chosen to risk the consequences of a life of action and danger, preferring the glory of achieving more than any King of Macedonia before him to a life of security. [16] But his subjects have no share in the honour and glory. Constantly battered about by all these expeditions, up and down, they are vexed with incessant hardships: they are not suffered to pursue their occupations or attend to their own affairs: for the little that they produce, as best they can, they can find no market, the trading stations of the country being closed on account of the war. [17] From these facts it is not difficult to discover the attitude of the Macedonians in general towards Philip; and as for the mercenaries and Infantry of the Guard who surround him, though they have the reputation of being a fine body of well-drilled warriors, I am told by a man who has been in Macedonia, and who is incapable of falsehood, that they are no better than any other body of men. [18] Granted that there may be experienced campaigners and fighters among them; yet, he tells me, Philip is so jealous of honour, that he thrusts all such men away from him, in his anxiety to get the credit of every achievement for himself; for in addition to all his other qualities, his jealousy is insurpassable. On the other hand, any generally temperate or upright man, who cannot endure the dissolute life there, day by day, nor the drunkenness and the lewd revels, is thrust on one side and counts for nothing. [19] Thus he is left with brigands and flatterers, and men who, when in their cups, indulge in dances of a kind which I shrink from naming to you now. And it is evident that this report is true; for men whom every one tried to drive out of Athens, as far viler than even the very juggler in the street—Callias the public slave and men like him, players of farces, composers of indecent songs, written at the expense of their companions in the hope of raising a laugh—these are the men he likes and keeps about him. [20] You may think that these are trivial things, men of Athens: but they are weighty, in the judgement of of every right-minded man, as illustrations of the temper with which Philip is cursed. At present, I suppose, these facts are overshadowed by his continual prosperity. Success has a wonderful power of throwing a veil over shameful things like these. But let him only stumble, and then all these features in his character will be displayed in their true light. And I believe, men of Athens, that the revelation is not far off, if Heaven be willing and you desirous of it. [21] So long as a man is in good health, he is unconscious of any weakness; but if any illness comes upon him, the disturbance affects every weak point, be it a rupture or a sprain or anything else that is unsound in his constitution. And as with the body, so it is with a city or a tyrant. So long as they are at war abroad, the mischief is hidden from the world at large, but the close grapple of war on the frontier brings all to light.

[22] Now if any of you, men of Athens, seeing Philip's good fortune, thinks that this makes him a formidable enemy to fight against, he reasons like a sensible man: for fortune weighs heavily in the scale—nay, fortune is everything, in all human affairs. And yet, if I were given the choice, it is the fortune of Athens that I should choose, rather than that of Philip, provided that you yourselves are willing to act even to a small extent as you should act. For I see that there are far more abundant grounds for expecting the goodwill of Heaven on your side than on his. [23] But here, of course, we are sitting idle; and one who is a sluggard himself cannot require his friends to help him, much less the gods. It is not to be wondered at that Philip, who goes on

ii. §22 His
fortune vs.
ours

iii. §§23–30
Our weak-
nesses are his
strength

campaigns and works hard himself, and is always at the scene of action, and lets no opportunity go, no season pass, should get the better of us who delay and pass resolutions and ask for news; nor do I wonder at it. It is the opposite that would have been wonderful—if we, who do nothing that those who are at war ought to do, were successful against one who leaves nothing undone. [24] But this I do wonder at, that you who once raised your hand against Sparta, in defence of the rights of the Hellenes—you, who with opportunities often open to you for grasping large advantages for yourselves, would not take them, but to secure for others their rights spent your own fortunes in war-contributions, and always bore the brunt of the dangers of the campaign—that you, I say, are now shrinking from marching, and hesitating to make any contribution to save your own possessions; and that, though you have often saved the rest of the Hellenes, now all together and now each in their turn, you are sitting idle, when you have lost what was your own. [25] I wonder at this; and I wonder also, men of Athens, that none of you is able to reckon up the time during which you have been fighting with Philip, and to consider what you have been doing while all this time has been going by. Surely you must know that it is while we have been delaying, hoping that some one else would act, accusing one another, bringing one another to trial, hoping anew—in fact, doing practically what we are doing now—that all the time has passed. [26] And have you now so little sense, men of Athens, as to hope that the very same policy, which has made the position of the city a bad one instead of a good, will actually make it a good one instead of a bad? Why, it is contrary both to reason and to nature to think so! It is always much easier to retain than to acquire. But now, owing to the war, none of our old possessions is left for us to retain; and so we must needs acquire. [27] This, therefore, is our own personal and immediate duty; and accordingly I say that you must contribute funds, you must go on service in person with a good will, you must accuse no one before you have become masters of the situation; and then you must honour those who deserve praise, and punish the guilty, with a judgement based upon the actual facts. You must get rid of all excuses and all deficiencies on your own part; you cannot examine mercilessly the actions of others, unless you yourselves have done all that your duty requires. [28] For why is it, do you think, men of Athens, that all the generals whom you dispatch avoid this war, and discover private wars of their own—if a little of the truth must be told even about the generals? It is because in this war the prizes for which the war is waged are yours, and if they are captured, you will take them immediately for your own; but the dangers are the personal privilege of your commanders, and no pay is forthcoming: while in those wars the dangers are less, and the profits— Lampsacus, Sigeum, and the ships which they plunder— go to the commanders and their men. Each force therefore takes the road that leads to its own advantage. [29] For your part, when you turn your attention to the serious condition of your affairs, you first bring the commanders to trial; and then, when you have given them a hearing, and have been told of the difficulties which I have described, you acquit them. The result, therefore, is that while you are quarrelling with one another and broken into factions—one party persuaded of this, another of that—the public interest suffers. You used, men of Athens, to pay taxes by Boards: to-day you conduct your politics by Boards. On either side there is an orator as leader, and a general under him; and for the Three Hundred, there are those who come to shout. The rest of you distribute yourselves between the two parties, some on either side. [30] This system you must give up:

The symmory boards, groups of citizens who contributed ships

65

you must even now become your own masters; you must give to all alike their share in discussion, in speech and in action. If you assign to one body of men the function of issuing orders to you, like tyrants; to another, that of compulsory service as trierarchs or tax-payers or soldiers; and to another, only that of voting their condemnation, without taking any share in the labour, nothing that ought to be done will be done in time. For the injured section will always be in default, and you will only have the privilege of punishing them instead of the enemy.

Summary, §31

[31] To sum up, all must contribute, each according to his wealth, in a fair proportion: all must go on active service in turn, until you have all served: you must give a hearing to all who come forward, and choose the best course out of all that you hear—not the course proposed by this or that particular person. If you do this, you will not only commend the proposer of that course at the time, but you will commend yourselves hereafter, for the whole position of your affairs will be a better one.

From the
ADDRESS TO PHILIP OF ISOCRATES

INTRODUCTION

Although both the *Second Olynthiac* of Demosthenes and the *Address to Philip* of Isocrates focus on the character and policies of Philip of Macedon, it is often hard to believe that they are discussing the same man. The despicable debauchee pictured in Demosthenes has metamorphosed himself into a capable and conscientious leader well qualified to carry out Isocrates' project, the Greek invasion of Persia. The man Demosthenes thought was a barbarian has become a Greek of the most distinguished genealogy. The enemy of Hellenic culture has become the man who could extend and invigorate it. In short, Demosthenes and Isocrates present totally different responses to the same undeniable fact, the emergence of Macedon as a major power in the Greek world.

It is this same fact that accounts for some of the changes that have taken place in Isocrates' project in the thirty-five years or so since he first set down in the *Panegyricus* his plan for the invasion of Asia. The idea is still the same, but he has a totally new conception of the organization needed to implement it. The *Panegyricus* concentrated on the two traditional leaders of Greece, Athens and Sparta, and mentioned Macedon only in passing. The *Address to Philip* beseeches the Macedonian king to lead the expedition, for Isocrates has abandoned his hope that Athens or any other Greek city could serve as an effective leader.

Thus Isocrates, like Demosthenes, attests the importance of the rise of Macedon as a new factor in Greek foreign relations. But unlike Demosthenes, Isocrates believes that this new power can cooperate with the city-states and ultimately strengthen and enrich all Greece. At the time of the publication of the *Address to Philip* this expectation had recently been encouraged by a peace which Athens and Macedon had agreed upon in 346 B.C., after ten years of sporadic fighting. This treaty, negotiated among others by Aeschines, a less than enthusiastic Demosthenes, and one Philocrates, after whom it is named, seemed to Isocrates to provide an auspicious opportunity for renewing his proposals for the attack on Persia. This is the primary purpose of the *Address to Philip* (346 B.C.) but at the same time by stressing that Philip was a true Greek and by calling attention to the possibility of cooperation with him Isocrates held out a constructive alternative to the policies of those who were anxious to discredit Philocrates, destroy the peace, and find some way to humiliate Philip. Isocrates could hope that even if his proposal was not adopted, he might yet help steer Athens away from a collision with Macedon.

Once again, as the next few speeches will make clear, the collision was not to be avoided. The Peace of Philocrates was more a truce than a lasting adjudication of conflicting interests. The few years' breathing space that it afforded was not used for serious negotiations and no understanding was reached between Athens and Macedon. Isocrates seems again to have spoken to deaf ears. But the speech he produced, apart from its substantial literary merits and the vigor of thought and style so remarkable in a man ninety years old, invites speculation about one of the most intriguing possibilities in the history of Greece. Here is an intelligent and by no means uninformed Athenian who challenges Demosthenes' assessment of Philip and proclaims the possibility of cooperation between Macedon and the rest of Greece.

The translation by George Norlin, former president of the University of Colorado, which is used here first appeared in the Loeb Classical Library in 1928. It aims at a different sort of accuracy from that sought by John Gillies in his *Panegyricus*. Norlin attempted, with some unavoidable exceptions, to translate sentence for sentence, denying himself the freedom to combine, expand, and compress that Gillies had so lavishly exercised. The result is a precise but perhaps pedestrian version which prefers an affectionate closeness to the Greek to the blandishments of English rhetoric.

———

Isocrates begins his speech by referring to Athens' dispute with Macedon over her old colony Amphipolis, an important trade and mining town in Thrace. It was a struggle for the control of this city that ten years earlier in 356 had led to the outbreak of hostilities between Philip and Athens. The recent peace negotiated by Philocrates and others was welcomed by Isocrates, but he points out it is not likely to endure unless

[9] the greatest states of Hellas should resolve to put an end to their mutual quarrels and carry the war beyond our borders into Asia, and should determine to wrest from the barbarians the advantages which they now think it proper to get for themselves at the expense of the Hellenes. This was, in fact, the course which I had already advocated in the *Panegyric* discourse.

[10] Having pondered these matters and come to the conclusion that there could never be found a subject nobler than this, of more general appeal, or of greater profit to us all, I was moved to write upon it a second time. Yet I did not fail to appreciate my own deficiencies; I knew that this theme called for a man, not of my years, 90 years old but in the full bloom of his vigour and with natural endowments far above those of other men; [11] and I realized also that it is difficult to deliver two discourses with tolerable success upon the same subject, especially when the one which was first published was so written that even my detractors imitate and admire it more than do those who praise it to excess. [12] Nevertheless, disregarding all these difficulties, I have become so ambitious in my old age that I have determined by address-

ing my discourse to you at the same time to set an example to my disciples and make it evident to them that to burden our national assemblies with oratory and to address all the people who there throng together is, in reality, to address no one at all; that such speeches are quite as ineffectual as the legal codes and constitutions drawn up by the sophists; [13] and, finally, that those who desire, not to chatter empty nonsense, but to further some practical purpose, and those who think they have hit upon some plan for the common good, must leave it to others to harangue at the public festivals, but must themselves win over someone to champion their cause from among men who are capable not only of speech but of action and who occupy a high position in the world—if, that is to say, they are to command any attention.

[14] It was with this mind then that I chose to address to you what I have to say—not that I singled you out to curry your favour, although in truth I would give much to speak acceptably to you. It was not, however, with this in view that I came to my decision, but rather because I saw that all the other men of high repute were living under the control of polities and laws, with no power to do anything save what was prescribed, and that, furthermore, they were sadly unequal to the enterprise which I shall propose; [15] while you and you alone had been granted by fortune free scope both to send ambassadors to whomsoever you desire and to receive them from whomsoever you please, and to say whatever you think expedient; and that, besides, you, beyond any of the Hellenes, were possessed of both wealth and power, which are the only things in the world that are adapted at once to persuade and to compel; and these aids, I think, even the cause which I shall propose to you will need to have on its side. [16] For I am going to advise you to champion the cause of concord among

Philip's free-
dom vs. Greek
constitutional
restrictions

70

the Hellenes and of a campaign against the barbarian; and as persuasion will be helpful in dealing with the Hellenes, so compulsion will be useful in dealing with the barbarians. This, then, is the general scope of my discourse. . . .

[30] I affirm that, without neglecting any of your own interests, you ought to make an effort to reconcile Argos and Lacedaemon and Thebes and Athens; for if you can bring these cities together, you will not find it hard to unite the others as well; [31] for all the rest are under the protection of the aforesaid cities, and fly for refuge, when they are alarmed, to one or other of these powers, and they all draw upon them for succour. So that if you can persuade four cities only to take a sane view of things, you will deliver the others also from many evils.

The proposal

[32] Now you will realize that it is not becoming in you to disregard any of these cities if you will review their conduct in relation to your ancestors; for you will find that each one of them is to be credited with great friendship and important services to your house: Argos is the land of your fathers, and is entitled to as much consideration at your hands as are your own ancestors; the Thebans honour the founder of your race, both by processionals and by sacrifices, beyond all the other gods; [33] the Lacedaemonians have conferred upon his descendants the kingship and the power of command for all time; and as for our city, we are informed by those whom we credit in matters of ancient history that she aided Heracles to win his immortality (in what way you can easily learn at another time; it would be unseasonable for me to relate it now), and that she aided his children to preserve their lives. [34] Yes, Athens single-handed sustained the greatest dangers against the power of Eurystheus, put an end to his insolence, and freed Heracles' sons from the fears by

The Greeks honor Philip's ancestor, Heracles

Cf. Lysias *Funeral Oration* §§11–16

71

which they were continually beset. Because of these services we deserve the gratitude, not only of those who then were preserved from destruction, but also of those who are now living; for to us it is due both that they are alive and that they enjoy the blessings which are now theirs, since they never could have seen the light of day at all had not the sons of Heracles been preserved from death.

[35] Therefore, seeing that these cities have each and all shown such a spirit, no quarrel should ever have arisen between you and any one of them. But unfortunately we are all prone by nature to do wrong more often than right; and so it is fair to charge the mistakes of the past to our common weakness. Yet for the future you must be on your guard to prevent a like occurrence, and must consider what service you can render them which will make it manifest that you have acted in a manner worthy both of yourself and of what these cities have done. [36] And the opportunity now serves you; for you would not only be repaying the debt of gratitude which you owed them, but, because so much time has elapsed, they will credit you with being first in friendly offices. And it is a good thing to have the appearance of conferring benefits upon the greatest states of Hellas and at the same time to profit yourself no less than them. [37] But apart from this, if anything unpleasant has arisen between you and any of them, you will wipe it out completely; for friendly acts in the present crisis will make you forget the wrongs which you have done each other in the past. Yes, and this also is beyond question, that all men hold in fondest memory those benefits which they receive in times of trouble. [38] And you see how utterly wretched these states have become because of their warfare, and how like they are to men engaged in a personal encounter; for no one can reconcile the parties to a quarrel while their wrath is rising; but after they

have punished each other badly, they need no mediator, but separate of their own accord. And that is just what I think these states also will do unless you first take them in hand.

[39] Now perhaps someone will venture to object to what I have proposed, saying that I am trying to persuade you to set yourself to an impossible task, since the Argives could never be friendly to the Lacedaemonians, nor the Lacedaemonians to the Thebans, and since, in general, those who have been accustomed throughout their whole existence to press their own selfish interests can never share and share alike with each other. [40] Well, I myself do not believe that at the time when our city was the first power in Hellas, or again when Lacedaemon occupied that position, any such result could have been accomplished, since the one or the other of these two cities could easily have blocked the attempt; but as things are now, I am not of the same mind regarding them. For I know that they have all been brought down to the same level by their misfortunes, and so I think that they would much prefer the mutual advantages which would come from a unity of purpose to the selfish gains which accrued from their policy in those days. [41] Furthermore, while I grant that no one else in the world could reconcile these cities, yet nothing of the sort is difficult for you; for I see that you have carried through to a successful end many undertakings which the rest of the world looked upon as hopeless and unthinkable, and therefore it would be nothing strange if you should be able single-handed to effect this union. In fact, men of high purposes and exceptional gifts ought not to undertake enterprises which any of the common run might carry out with success, but rather those which no one would attempt save men with endowments and power such as you possess.

[42] But I marvel that those who think that none of

The period of Athenian dominance 477–405 B.C.

these proposals could possibly be carried out are not aware, either by their own knowledge or by tradition, that there have been many terrible wars after which the participants have come to an understanding and rendered great services to one another. For what could exceed the enmity which the Hellenes felt toward Xerxes? Yet everyone knows that we and the Lacedaemonians came to prize his friendship more than that of those who helped us to establish our respective empires. [43] But why speak of ancient history, or of our dealings with the barbarians? If one should scan and review the misfortunes of the Hellenes in general, these will appear as nothing in comparison with those which we Athenians have experienced through the Thebans and the Lacedaemonians. Nevertheless, when the Lacedaemonians took the field against the Thebans and were minded to humiliate Boeotia and break up the league of her cities, we sent a relief expedition and thwarted the desires of the Lacedaemonians. [44] And again, when fortune shifted her favour and the Thebans and the Peloponnesians were one and all trying to devastate Lacedaemon, we alone among the Hellenes formed an alliance with the Lacedaemonians and helped to save them from destruction. [45] So then, seeing that such great reversals are wont to occur, and that our states care nothing about their former enmities or about their oaths or about anything else save what they conceive to be expedient for themselves, and that expediency is the sole object to which they give their affections and devote all their zeal, no man, unless obsessed by utter folly, could fail to believe that now also they will show the same disposition, especially if you take the lead in their reconciliation, while selfish interests urge and present ills constrain them to this course. I, for my part, believe that, with these influences fighting on your side, everything will turn out as it should.

E.g., the disasters of the Peloponnesian War, 431–404 B.C.

378 B.C.

370–69 B.C.

[46] But I think that you can get most light on the question whether these cities are inclined toward peace with each other or toward war, if I review, not merely in general terms nor yet with excessive detail, the principal facts in their present situation. And first of all, let us consider the condition of the Lacedaemonians.

[47] The Lacedaemonians were the leaders of the Hellenes, not long ago, on both land and sea, and yet they suffered so great a reversal of fortune when they met defeat at Leuctra that they were deprived of their power over the Hellenes, and lost such of their warriors as chose to die rather than survive defeat at the hands of those over whom they had once been masters. [48] Furthermore, they were obliged to look on while all the Peloponnesians, who formerly had followed the lead of Lacedaemon against the rest of the world, united with the Thebans and invaded their territory; and against these the Lacedaemonians were compelled to risk battle, not in the country to save the crops, but in the heart of the city, before the very seat of their government, to save their wives and children—a crisis in which defeat meant instant destruction, [49] and victory has none the more delivered them from their ills; nay, they are now warred upon by their neighbours; they are distrusted by all the Peloponnesians; they are hated by most of the Hellenes; they are harried and plundered day and night by their own serfs; and not a day passes that they do not have to take the field or fight against some force or other, or march to the rescue of their perishing comrades. [50] But the worst of their afflictions is that they live in continual fear that the Thebans may patch up their quarrel with the Phocians and, returning again, ring them about with still greater calamities than have befallen them in the past. How, then, can we refuse to believe that people so hard pressed would gladly see at the head of a movement for peace a man who commands

The period of Spartan dominance, 405–371 B.C.

The campaigns of Epaminondas, 371–62 B.C.

75

confidence and has the power to put an end to the wars in which they are involved?

[51] Now as to the Argives, you will see that in some respects they are no better off than the Lacedaemonians, while in others their condition is worse; for they have been in a state of war with their neighbours from the day they founded their city, just as have the Lacedaemonians; but there is this difference, that the neighbours of the Lacedaemonians are weaker than they, while those of the Argives are stronger—a condition which all would admit to be the greatest of misfortunes. And so unsuccessful are they in their warfare that hardly a year passes that they are not compelled to witness their own territory being ravaged and laid waste. [52] But what is most deplorable of all is that, during the intervals when their enemies cease from harrying them, they themselves put to death the most eminent and wealthy of their citizens; and they have more pleasure in doing this than any other people have in slaying their foes. The cause of their living in such disorder is none other than the state of war; and if you can put a stop to this, you will not only deliver them from these evils but you will cause them to adopt a better policy with respect to their other interests as well.

[53] And as for the condition of the Thebans, surely you have not failed to note that also. They won a splendid victory and covered themselves with glory, but because they did not make good use of their success they are now in no better case than those who have suffered defeat and failure. For no sooner had they triumphed over their foes than, neglecting everything else, they began to annoy the cities of the Peloponnese; they made bold to reduce Thessaly to subjection; they threatened their neighbours, the Megarians; they robbed our city of a portion of its territory; they ravaged Euboea; they sent men-of-war to Byzantium as if they purposed to rule

Argos and her
neighbours,
e.g., Sparta

Thebes' vic-
tory at Leuc-
tra, 371 B.C.

both land and sea; [54] and, finally, they began war upon the Phocians, expecting that in a short time they would conquer their cities, occupy all the surrounding territory, and prevail over all the treasures at Delphi by the outlay of their own funds. But none of these hopes has been realized; instead of seizing the cities of the Phocians they have lost cities of their own; and now when they invade the enemy's territory they inflict less damage upon them than they suffer when they are retreating to their own country; [55] for while they are in Phocian territory they succeed in killing a few hireling soldiers who are better off dead than alive, but when they retreat they lose of their own citizens those who are most esteemed and most ready to die for their fatherland. And so completely have their fortunes shifted, that whereas they once hoped that all Hellas would be subject to them, now they rest upon you the hopes of their own deliverance. Therefore I think that the Thebans also will do with alacrity whatever you command or advise.

Thebes' aggressive behavior, 369–46 B.C.

[56] It would still remain for me to speak about our city, had she not come to her senses before the others and made peace; but now I need only say this: I think that she will join forces with you in carrying out your policy, especially if she can be made to see that your object is to prepare for the campaign against the barbarians. . . .

Athens

[68] Consider how worthy a thing it is to undertake, above all, deeds of such a character that if you succeed you will cause your own reputation to rival that of the foremost men of history, while if you fall short of your expectations you will at any rate win the good will of all the Hellenes—which is a better thing to gain than to take by force many Hellenic cities; for achievements of the latter kind entail envy and hostility and much opprobrium, but that which I have urged entails none of these things. Nay, if some god were to give you the choice of

An appeal to Philip's pride

the interests and the occupations in which you would
wish to spend your life, you could not, at least if you took
my advice, choose any in preference to this; [69] for you
will not only be envied of others, but you will also count
yourself a happy man. For what good fortune could
then surpass your own? Men of the highest renown will
come as ambassadors from the greatest states to your
court; you will advise with them about the general welfare, for which no other man will be found to have
shown a like concern; [70] you will see all Hellas on tip-
toe with interest in whatever you happen to propose;
and no one will be indifferent to the measures which
are being decided in your councils, but, on the contrary,
some will seek news of how matters stand, some will
pray that you will not be thwarted in your aims, and
others will fear lest something befall you before your
efforts are crowned with success. [71] If all this should
come to pass, would you not have good reason to be
proud? Would you not rejoice throughout your life in
the knowledge that you had been a leader in such great
affairs? And what man that is even moderately endowed
with reason would not exhort you to fix your choice
above all upon that course of action which is capable of
bearing at one and the same time the twofold fruits, if
I may so speak, of surpassing joys and of imperishable
honours?

[72] Now I should content myself with what I have
already said on this topic, had I not passed over a certain matter—not that it slipped my memory, but because
I hesitated to speak of it—which I am now resolved to
disclose to you. For I think that it is profitable for you
to hear about it, and that it is becoming in me to speak,
as I am wont to do, without reserve.

[73] I observe that you are being painted in false
colours by men who are jealous of you, for one thing,
and are, besides, in the habit of stirring up trouble in

their own cities—men who look upon a state of peace which is for the good of all as a state of war upon their selfish interests. Heedless of all other considerations, they keep talking about your power, representing that it is being built up, not in behalf of Hellas, but against her, that you have for a long time been plotting against us all, [74] and that, while you are giving it out that you intend to go to the rescue of the Messenians, if you can settle the Phocian question, you really design to subdue the Peloponnesus to your rule. The Thessalians, they say, and the Thebans, and all those who belong to the Amphictyony, stand ready to follow your lead; while the Argives, the Messenians, the Megalopolitans, and many of the others are prepared to join forces with you and wipe out the Lacedaemonians; and if you succeed in doing this, you will easily be master of the rest of Hellas. [75] By speaking this rubbish, by pretending to have exact knowledge and by speedily effecting in words the overthrow of the whole world, they are convincing many people. They convince, most of all, those who hunger for the same calamities as do the speechmakers; next, those who exercise no judgement about their common welfare, but, utterly obtuse in their own perceptions, are very grateful to men who pretend to feel alarm and fear in their behalf; and lastly, those who do not deny that you appear to be plotting against the Hellenes, but are of the opinion that the purpose with which you are charged is a worthy ambition.

[76] For these latter are so far divorced from intelligence that they do not realize that one may apply the same words in some cases to a man's injury, in others to his advantage. For example, if at the present moment one were to say that the King of Asia was plotting against the Hellenes, and had made preparations to send an expedition against us, he would not be saying anything disparaging of him; nay, he would, on the contrary, make us

Slanders
against
Philip

His support of
the Delphic
Amphictyony
merely a pre-
liminary to an
attack on
Sparta

think more highly of his courage and his worth. But if, on the other hand, one should bring this charge against one of the descendants of Heracles, who made himself the benefactor of all Hellas, he would bring upon him the greatest opprobrium. [77] For who would not feel indignation and loathing if a man should be found to be plotting against those in whose behalf his ancestor elected to live a life of perils, and if he made no effort to preserve the good will which the latter had bequeathed as a legacy to his posterity, but, heedless of these examples, set his heart on reprehensible and wicked deeds?

E.g., Philip

[78] You ought to give these matters careful thought, and not look on with indifference while rumours are springing up around you of the sort which your enemies seek to fasten upon you, but which your friends, to a man, would not hesitate to deny. And yet it is in the feelings of both these parties that you can best see the truth as to your own interests. [79] Perhaps, however, you conceive that it argues a mean spirit to pay attention to the drivellers who heap abuse upon you and to those who are influenced by what they say, especially when your own conscience is free from any sense of guilt. But you ought not to despise the multitude nor count it a little thing to have the respect of the whole world; on the contrary, you ought then, and only then, to be satisfied that you enjoy a reputation which is good and great and worthy of yourself and of your forefathers and of the achievements of your line, [80] when you have brought the Hellenes to feel toward you as you see the Lacedaemonians feel toward their kings, and as your companions feel toward yourself. And it is not difficult for you to attain this if you determine to show yourself equally friendly to all, and cease treating some of the cities as friends and others as strangers, and if, furthermore, you fix your choice upon the kind of policy by which you can make yourself trusted by the Hellenes and feared by the barbarians.

A gentle criticism

After a brief interlude in which he discusses his personal qualifications for proposing such an expedition, Isocrates turns to the strategic prerequisites for a successful invasion of Persia:

[86] The point of departure, then, which I have taken for my whole discussion is, I believe, the one which is proper for those who urge an expedition against Asia. For one must undertake nothing until he finds the Hellenes doing one of two things: either actually supporting the undertaking or according it their entire approval. . . . [89] On these points no man of intelligence would venture to contradict me. But I think that if any of the others should be prompted to advise you in favour of the expedition against Asia, they would resort to a plea of this kind: that it has been the fortune of all who have undertaken a war against the King, without exception, to rise from obscurity to brilliant distinction, from poverty to wealth, and from low estate to be masters of many lands and cities. [90] I, however, am not going to urge you on such grounds, but by the example of men who were looked upon as failures: I mean those who took the field with Cyrus and Clearchus.

Argument by example

Everyone agrees that these won as complete a victory in battle over all the forces of the King as if they had come to blows with their womenfolk, but that at the very moment when they seemed to be masters of the field they failed of success, owing to the impetuosity of Cyrus. For he in his exultation rushed in pursuit far in advance of the others; and, being caught in the midst of the enemy, was killed. [91] But the King, notwithstanding that his foes had suffered so severe a loss, felt so thorough a contempt for his own forces that he invited Clearchus and the other captains to a parley, promising to give them great gifts and to pay their soldiers their wages in full and to give them safe convoy home; then, having lured them by such prospects,

The Greek troops hired by Cyrus, 401–399 B.C.

Compare
Xenophon's
Anabasis

and having assured them by the most solemn pledges
known to the Persians, he seized them and put them to
death, deliberately choosing to outrage the gods rather
than risk a clash with our soldiers, bereft though they
now were of Cyrus's aid. [92] And what challenge could
be nobler or more convincing than this? For it is evident that, if it had not been for Cyrus, even that army
would have overthrown the power of the King. But for
you it is easy both to guard against the disaster which
befell at that time and to equip yourself with an armament much stronger than that which defeated the forces
of the King. How, then, since you possess both these
advantages, can you fail to undertake this expedition
with all confidence? . . .

[95] Therefore, as next in order I think that I
should speak of the war-strength which will be avail-
Compare §80 able to you as compared with that which Clearchus and
his followers had. First and most important of all, you
will have the good will of the Hellenes if you choose to
abide by the advice which I have given you concerning
them; they, on the other hand, found the Hellenes in-
tensely hostile because of the decarchies which the
Lacedaemonians had set up; for the Hellenes thought
that, if Cyrus and Clearchus should succeed, their yoke
would be heavier still, but that if the King conquered
they would be delivered from their present hardships;
and this is just what did happen to them. [96] Besides,
you will find as many soldiers at your service as you wish,
Availability
of mercenaries for such is now the state of affairs in Hellas that it is
easier to get together a greater and stronger army from
among those who wander in exile than from those who
live under their own polities. But in those days there was
no body of professional soldiers, and so, being compelled
to collect mercenaries from the several states, they had
to spend more money on bounties for their recruiting
agents than on pay for the troops. [97] And, lastly, if

we should be inclined to make a careful review of the two cases and institute a comparison between you, who are to be at the head of the present expedition and to decide on every measure, and Clearchus, who was in charge of the enterprise of that day, we should find that he had never before been in command of any force whatever on either land or sea and yet attained renown from the misfortune which befell him on the continent of Asia; [98] while you, on the contrary, have succeeded in so many and such mighty achievements that if I were making them the subject of a speech before another audience, I should do well to recount them, but, since I am addressing myself to you, you would rightly think it senseless and gratuitous in me to tell you the story of your own deeds. [99] It is well for me to speak to you also about the two Kings, the one against whom I am advising you to take the field, and the one against whom Clearchus made war, in order that you may know the temper and the power of each. In the first place, the father of the present King once defeated our city and later the city of the Lacedaemonians, while this King has never overcome anyone of the armies which have been violating his territory. [100] Secondly, the former took the whole of Asia from the Hellenes by the terms of the Treaty; while this King is so far from exercising dominion over others that he is not in control even of the cities which were surrendered to him; and such is the state of affairs that there is no one who is not in doubt what to believe—whether he has given them up because of his cowardice, or whether they have learned to despise and contemn the power of the barbarians.

[101] Consider the state of affairs in his empire. Who could hear the facts and not be spurred to war against him? Egypt was, it is true, in revolt even when Cyrus made his expedition; but her people nevertheless were living in continual fear lest the King might some day

Artaxerxes II, ruled 404–358 B.C.

Artaxerxes III, ruled 358–38 B.C.

The King's Peace of 386 B.C.

lead an army in person and overcome the natural obstacles which, thanks to the Nile, their country presents, and all their military defences as well. But now this King has delivered them from that dread; for after he had brought together and fitted out the largest force he could possibly raise and marched against them, he retired from Egypt not only defeated, but laughed at and scorned as unfit either to be a king or to command an army. [102] Furthermore, Cyprus and Phoenicia and Cilicia, and that region from which the barbarians used to recruit their fleet, belonged at that time to the King, but now they have either revolted from him or are so involved in war and its attendant ills that none of these peoples is of any use to him; while to you, if you desire to make war upon him, they will be serviceable. [103] And mark also that Idrieus, who is the most prosperous of the present rulers of the mainland, must in the nature of things be more hostile to the interests of the King than are those who are making open war against him; verily he would be of all men the most perverse if he did not desire the dissolution of that empire which outrages his brother, which made war upon himself, and which at all times has never ceased to plot against him in its desire to be master of his person and of all his wealth. [104] It is through fear of these things that he is now constrained to pay court to the King and to send him much tribute every year; but if you should cross over to the mainland with an army, he would greet you with joy, in the belief that you were come to his relief; and you will also induce many of the other satraps to throw off the King's power if you promise them "freedom" and scatter broadcast over Asia that word which, when sown among the Hellenes, has broken up both our empire and that of the Lacedaemonians.

In a brief excursus on the Macedonian royal family Isocrates points out that an invasion of Persia

Marginal notes:

Failure of Artaxerxes' Egyptian campaign of 351 B.C.

Affairs in Caria

Mausolus, ruler of Caria, died 353 B.C.

would be in keeping with the traditions of Philip's ancestors. He even discusses the successes achieved against the barbarians by the mythical founder of Philip's line, Heracles.

[114] I do not mean that you will be able to imitate Heracles in all his exploits; for even among the gods there are some who could not do that; but in the qualities of the spirit, in devotion to humanity, and in the good will which he cherished toward the Hellenes, you can come close to his purposes. And it lies in your power, if you will heed my words, to attain whatever glory you yourself desire; [115] for it is easier for you to rise from your present station and win the noblest fame than it has been to advance from the station which you inherited to the fame which is now yours. And mark that I am summoning you to an undertaking in which you will make expeditions, not with the barbarians against men who have given you no just cause, but with the Hellenes against those upon whom it is fitting that the descendants of Heracles should wage war. . . .

Further comparison of Philip to Heracles

[119] From many considerations you ought to act in this way, but especially from the experiences of Jason. For he, without having achieved anything comparable to what you have done, won the highest renown, not from what he did, but from what he said; for he kept talking as if he intended to cross over to the continent and make war upon the King. [120] Now since Jason by use of words alone advanced himself so far, what opinion must we expect the world will have of you if you actually do this thing; above all, if you undertake to conquer the whole empire of the King, or, at any rate, to wrest from it a vast extent of territory and sever from it —to use a current phrase—"Asia from Cilicia to Sinope"; and if, furthermore, you undertake to establish cities in this region, and to settle in permanent abodes those who now, for lack of the daily necessities of life, are

Jason, tyrant of Pherae, ruled circa 380–70 B.C.

wandering from place to place and committing outrages upon whomsoever they encounter? [121] If we do not

Social unrest

stop these men from banding together, by providing sufficient livelihood for them, they will grow before we know it into so great a multitude as to be a terror no less to the Hellenes than to the barbarians. But we pay no heed to them; nay, we shut our eyes to the fact that a terrible menace which threatens us all alike is waxing day by day. [122] It is therefore the duty of a man who is high-minded, who is a lover of Hellas, who has a broader vision than the rest of the world, to employ these bands in a war against the barbarians, to strip from that empire all the territory which I defined a moment ago, to deliver these homeless wanderers from the ills by which they are afflicted and which they inflict upon others, to collect them into cities, and with these cities to fix the boundary of Hellas, making of them buffer states to shield us all. [123] For by doing this, you will not only make them prosperous, but you will put us all on a footing of security. If, however, you do not succeed in these objects, this much you will at any rate easily accomplish,—the liberation of the cities which are on the coast of Asia. . . .

[127] Nevertheless, since the others are so lacking in spirit, I think it is opportune for you to head the war against the King; and, while it is only natural for the other descendants of Heracles, and for men who are under the bonds of their polities and laws, to cleave fondly to that state in which they happen to dwell, it is your privilege, as one who has been blessed with untrammelled freedom, to consider all Hellas your fatherland, as did the founder of your race, and to be as ready to brave perils for her sake as for the things about which you are personally most concerned. [128] Perhaps there are those—men capable of nothing else but criticism—who will venture to rebuke me because I have chosen to

challenge you to the task of leading the expedition against the barbarians and of taking Hellas under your care, while I have passed over my own city. [129] Well, if I were trying to present this matter to any others before having broached it to my own country, which has thrice freed Hellas—twice from the barbarians and once from the Lacedaemonian yoke—I should confess my error. In truth, however, it will be found that I turned to Athens first of all and endeavoured to win her over to this cause with all the earnestness of which my nature is capable, but when I perceived that she cared less for what I said than for the ravings of the platform orators, I gave her up, although I did not abandon my efforts. [130] Wherefore I might justly be praised on every hand, because throughout my whole life I have constantly employed such powers as I possess in warring on the barbarians, in condemning those who opposed my plan, and in striving to arouse to action whomever I think will best be able to benefit the Hellenes in any way or to rob the barbarians of their present prosperity. [131] Consequently, I am now addressing myself to you, although I am not unaware that when I am proposing this course many will look at it askance, but that when you are actually carrying it out all will rejoice in it; for no one has had any part in what I have proposed, but when the benefits from it shall have been realized in fact, everyone without fail will look to have his portion.

[132] Consider what disgrace it is to sit idly and see Asia flourishing more than Europe and the barbarians enjoying a greater prosperity than the Hellenes; and, what is more, to see those who derive their power from Cyrus, who as a child was cast out by his mother on the public highway, addressed by the title of "The Great King," while the descendants of Heracles, who because of his virtue was exalted by his father to the rank of a god, are addressed by meaner titles than they. We must not

490 B.C.
Marathon

480 B.C.
Salamis

394 B.C.
Cnidus

The prosperity of Asia

87

allow this state of affairs to go on; no, we must change and reverse it entirely. [133] Rest assured that I should never have attempted to persuade you to undertake this at all had power and wealth been the only things which I saw would come of it; for I think that you' already have more than enough of such things, and that any man is beyond measure insatiable who deliberately chooses the extreme hazard of either winning these prizes or losing his life. [134] No, it is not with a view to the acquisition of wealth and power that I urge this course, but in the belief that by means of these you will win a name of surpassing greatness and glory. Bear in mind that while we all possess bodies that are mortal, yet by virtue of good will and praise and good report and memory which keeps pace with the passage of time we partake of im-

Immortality mortality—a boon for which we may well strive with all our might and suffer any hardship whatsoever. [135] You may observe that even common citizens of the best sort, who would exchange their lives for nothing else, are willing for the sake of winning glory to lay them down in battle; and, in general, that those who crave always an honour greater than they already possess are praised by all men, while those who are insatiable with regard to any other thing under the sun are looked upon as intemperate and mean. [136] But more important than all that I have said is the truth that wealth and positions of power often fall into the hands of our foes, whereas the good will of our fellow-countrymen and the other rewards which I have mentioned are possessions to which none can fall heir but our own children, and they alone. I could not, therefore, respect myself if I failed to advance these motives in urging you to make this expedition and wage war and brave its perils. . . .

Conclusion [149] Now if, after examining and reviewing all these admonitions in your own mind, you feel that my discourse is in any part rather weak and inadequate, set it down to my age, which might well claim the indulgence of all; but if it is up to the standard of my former publications, I would have you believe that it was not my old age that conceived it but the divine will that prompted it, not out of solicitude for me, but because of its concern for Hellas, and because of its desire to deliver her out of her present distress and to crown you with a glory far greater than you now possess. [150] I think that you are not unaware in what manner the gods order the affairs of mortals: for not with their own hands do they deal out the blessings and curses that befall us; rather they inspire in each of us such a state of mind [151] that good or ill, as the case may be, is visited upon us through one another. For example, it may be that even now the gods have assigned to me the task of speech while to you they allot the task of action, considering that you will be the best master in that province, while in the field of speech I might prove least irksome to my hearers. Indeed, I believe that even your past achievements would never have reached such magnitude had not one of the gods helped you to succeed; and I believe he did so, [152] not that you might spend your whole life warring upon the barbarians in Europe alone, but that, having been trained and having gained experience and come to know your own powers in these campaigns, you might set your heart upon the course which I have urged upon you. It were therefore shameful, now that fortune nobly leads the way, to lag behind and refuse to follow whither she desires to lead you forward.

[153] It is my belief that, while you ought to honour everyone who has any praise for your past accomplishments, you ought to consider that those laud you in the noblest terms who judge your nature capable of even greater triumphs, and not those whose discourse has gratified you for the moment only, but those who will cause future generations to admire your achievements

beyond the deeds of any man of the generations that are past. I would like to say many things in this strain, but I am not able; the reason why, I have stated more often than I ought.

[154] It remains, then, to summarize what I have said in this discourse, in order that you may see in the smallest compass the substance of my counsels. I assert that it is incumbent upon you to work for the good of the Hellenes, to reign as king over the Macedonians, and to extend your power over the greatest possible number of the barbarians. For if you do these things, all men will be grateful to you: the Hellenes for your kindness to them; the Macedonians if you reign over them, not like a tyrant, but like a king; and the rest of the nations, if by your hands they are delivered from barbaric despotism and are brought under the protection of Hellas.

[155] How well this discourse has been composed with respect to appropriateness and finish of style is a question which it is fair to ask my hearers to answer; but that no one could give you better advice than this, or advice more suited to the present situation—of this I believe that I am well assured.

THE THIRD PHILIPPIC OF DEMOSTHENES

INTRODUCTION

The Peace of Philocrates (346 B.C.), which Isocrates had hoped might bring about an era of cooperation between Athens and Macedon, was followed by six years of steady diplomatic calefaction as cold war turned slowly to hot. At first the problems were small. Philip, noticing that the peace specified that the parties were to keep the territory they held at the time of swearing, delayed taking the oath until he conquered two tiny towns in Thrace, Serrhium and Doriscus (§ 15). Then, once the peace was concluded, he moved unexpectedly, though quite legally, into north central Greece and settled a long-standing Amphictyonic dispute by expelling the Phocians from the sacred federation, taking for himself their seats in the council meeting, and imposing an indemnity for the treasure they had removed from the temple at Delphi. Soon Athens detected what she regarded as Philip's intrigues against her in the Peloponnese and on Euboea, an island only a few miles off her north eastern shore. Her fears grew as an expedition in Thrace brought Philip ever nearer the Chersonese and the Hellespont, places whose loss Athens could not afford to risk. Her response was to send the general Diopeithes and a band of mercenaries to oppose and harass Philip (341 B.C.); these, once they had reached Thrace, proceeded to attack Philip's ally Cardia—the first clear violation of the peace. Despite Philip's protests Athens with Demosthenes' encouragement refused to apologize or to discipline Diopeithes.

In this atmosphere of growing tension and bitterness (341 B.C.) Demosthenes came forward to deliver his *Third Philippic*, a speech whose compressed passion and distilled fury were well calculated to dissolve the final vestiges of peace. In it he blends all the noxious ingredients of the rhetorician's craft—slander, misrepresentation, appeals to Athens' pride, bitter reminiscences of her past grievances, warnings of subversion, and that favorite argument of those who wish war, the assurance that peace is already dead (§8). Demosthenes' policy and his ten years of sustained attack on Philip soon bore fruit as in the next years a diplomatic offensive, a struggle for the Hellespont, and the outbreak of war in Greece followed one after another. The *Third Philippic* thus marks an important stage in Demosthenes' oratorical effort against Philip, and embodies the very opposite of Isocrates' views and policies.

In a few places the margins of the best manuscripts of this speech contain passages which seem to be alternatives or supplements to the main text. Since these marginalia, which are also found in many inferior manuscripts, may represent parts of an alternative version of the speech produced in Demosthenes' own day, they are printed here, though separated from the rest of the text by square brackets.

---

[1] Many speeches are made, men of Athens, at almost every meeting of the Assembly, with reference to the aggressions which Philip has been committing, ever since he concluded the Peace, not only against yourselves but against all other peoples; and I am sure that all would agree, however little they may act on their belief, that our aim, both in speech and in action, should be to cause him to cease from his insolence and to pay the penalty for it. And yet I see that in fact the treacherous sacrifice of our interests has gone on, until what seems an ill-omened saying may, I fear, be really true—that if all who came forward desired to propose, and you desired to carry, the measures which would make your position as pitiful as it could possibly be, it could not (so I believe), be made worse than it is now. [2] It may be that there are many reasons for this, and that our affairs did not reach their present condi-

The Peace of
Philocrates,
346 B.C.

tion from any one or two causes. But if you examine the matter aright, you will find that the chief responsibility rests with those whose aim is to win your favour, not to propose what is best. Some of them, men of Athens, so long as they can maintain the conditions which bring them reputation and influence, take no thought for the future [and therefore think that you also should take none] while others, by accusing and slandering those who are actively at work, are simply trying to make the city spend its energies in punishing the members of its own body, and so leave Philip free to say and do what he likes. [3] Such political methods as these, familiar to you as they are, are the real causes of the evil. And I beg you, men of Athens, if I tell you certain truths outspokenly, to let no resentment on your part fall upon me on this account. Consider the matter in this light. In every other sphere of life, you believe that the right of free speech ought to be so universally shared by all who are in the city, that you have extended it both to foreigners and to slaves; and one may see many a servant in Athens speaking his mind with greater liberty than is granted to citizens in some other states: but from the sphere of political counsel you have utterly banished this liberty. [4] The result is that in your meetings you give yourselves airs and enjoy their flattery, listening to nothing but what is meant to please you, while in the world of facts and events, you are in the last extremity of peril. If then you are still in this mood to-day, I do not know what I can say; but if you are willing to listen while I tell you, without flattery, what your interest requires, I am prepared to speak. For though our position is very bad indeed, and much has been sacrificed, it is still possible, even now, if you will do your duty, to set all right once more. [5] It is a strange thing, perhaps, that I am about to say, but it is true. The worst feature in the past is that in which lies our best hope for the future. And what is this? It is that you are in your present plight because you do not do any part of your duty, small or great; for of course, if you were doing all that you should do, and were still in this evil case, you could not even hope for any improvement. As it is, Philip has conquered your indolence and your indifference; but he has not conquered Athens. You have not been vanquished—you have never even stirred.

[6] [Now if it was admitted by us all that Philip was at war with Athens, and was transgressing the Peace, a speaker would have to do nothing but to advise you as to the safest and easiest method of resistance to him. But since there are some who are in so extraordinary a frame of mind that, though he is capturing cities, though many of your possessions are in his hands, and though he is committing aggressions against all men, they still tolerate certain speakers, who constantly assert at your meetings that it is some of *us* who are provoking the war, it is necessary to be on our guard and come to a right understanding on the matter. [7] For there is a danger lest any one who proposes or advises resistance should find himself accused of having brought about the war.]

E.g., Philip's intrigues on Euboea

[Well, I say this first of all, and lay it down as a principle, that if it is open to us to deliberate whether we should remain at peace or should go to war . . .]

Now if it is possible for the city to remain at peace— if the [8] decision rests with us (that I may make this my starting-point)—then, I say that we ought to do so, and I call upon any one who says that it is so to move his motion, and to act and not to defraud us. But if another with weapons in his hands and a large force about him holds out to you the *name* of peace, while his own acts are acts of war, what course remains open to us but that of resistance? though if you wish to profess peace in the same manner as he, I have no quarrel with you. [9] But if any man's conception of peace is that it is a state in which Philip can master all that intervenes till at last he comes to attack ourselves, such a conception, in the first place, is madness; and, in the second place, this peace that he speaks of is a peace which you are to observe towards Philip, while he does not observe it towards you: and this it is—this power to carry on war against you, without being met by any hostilities on your part—that Philip is purchasing with all the money that he is spending.

[10] Indeed, if we intend to wait till the time comes when he admits that he is at war with us, we are surely the most innocent persons in the world. Why, even if he comes to Attica itself, to the very Peiraeus, he will never make such an admission, if we are to judge by his dealings with others. [11] For, to take one instance, he told the Olynthians, when he was five miles from the city, that there were only two alternatives—either they must cease to live in Olynthus, or he to live in Macedonia: but during the whole time before that, whenever any one accused him of any such sentiments, he was indignant and sent envoys to answer the charge. Again, he marched into the Phocians' country, as though visiting his allies: it was by Phocian envoys that he was escorted on the march; and most people in Athens contended strongly that his crossing the Pass would bring no good to Thebes. [12] Worse still, he has lately seized Pherae and still holds it, though he went to Thessaly as a friend and an ally. And, latest of all, he told those unhappy citizens of Oreus that he had sent his soldiers to visit them and to make kind inquiries; he had heard that they were sick, and suffering from faction, and it was right for an ally and a true friend to be present at such a time. [13] Now if, instead of giving them warning and using open force, he deliber-

348 B.C.

Philip overcomes the Phocians, 346 B.C.

343 B.C.

The democracy of Oreus in Euboea overthrown, 343 B.C.

ately chose to deceive these men, who could have done him no harm, though they might have taken precautions against suffering any themselves, do you imagine that he will make a formal declaration of war upon you before he commences hostilities, and that, so long as you are content to be deceived? [14] Impossible! For so long as you, though you are the injured party, make no complaint against him, but accuse some of your own body, he would be the most fatuous man on earth if *he* were to interrupt your strife and contentions with one another—to bid you turn upon himself, and so to cut away the ground from the arguments by which his hirelings put you off, when they tell you that *he* is not at war with Athens.

[15] In God's name, is there a man in his senses who would judge by words, and not by facts, whether another was at peace or at war with him? Of course there is not. Why, from the very first, when the Peace had only just been made, before those who are now in the Chersonese had been sent out, Philip was taking Serrhium and Doriscus, and expelling the soldiers who were in the castle of Serrhium and the Sacred Mountain, where they had been placed by your general. [16] But what was he doing, in acting thus? For he had sworn to a Peace. And let no one ask, 'What do these things amount to? What do they matter to Athens?' For whether these acts were trifles which could have no interest for you is another matter; but the principles of religion and justice, whether a man transgress them in small things or great, have always the same force. What? When he is sending mercenaries into the Chersonese, which the king and all the Hellenes have acknowledged to be yours; when he openly avows that he is going to the rescue, and states it in his letter, what is it that he is doing? [17] He tells you, indeed, that he is not making war upon you. But so far am I from admitting that one

Places in Thrace Philip seized before he swore to the Peace, 346 B.C.

96

who acts in this manner is observing the Peace which he made with you, that I hold that in grasping at Megara, in setting up tyrants in Euboea, in advancing against Thrace at the present moment, in pursuing his machinations in the Peloponnese, and in carrying out his entire policy with the help of his army, he is violating the Peace and is making war against you;—unless you mean to say that even to bring up engines to besiege you is no breach of the Peace, until they are actually planted against your walls. But you will not say this; for the man who is taking the steps and contriving the means which will lead to my capture is at war with me, even though he has not yet thrown a missile or shot an arrow. [18] Now what are the things which would imperil your safety, if anything should happen? The alienation of the Hellespont, the placing of Megara and Euboea in the power of the enemy, and the attraction of Peloponnesian sympathy to his cause. Can I then say that one who is erecting such engines of war as these against the city is at peace with you? [19] Far from it! For from the very day when he annihilated the Phocians—from that very day, I say, I date the beginning of his hostilities against you. And for your part, I think that you will be wise if you resist him at once; but that if you let him be, you will find that, when you wish to resist, resistance itself is impossible. Indeed, so widely do I differ, men of Athens, from all your other advisers, that I do not think there is any room for discussion to-day in regard to the Chersonese or Byzantium. [20] We *must* go to their defence, and take every care that they do not suffer [and we must send all that they need to the soldiers who are at present there]. But we *have* to take counsel for the good of all the Hellenes, in view of the grave peril in which they stand. And I wish to tell you on what grounds I am so alarmed at the situation, in order that

Philip's subversion in Megara and Euboea, 343 B.C.

What if war were actually declared?

Immediately after the Peace in 346 B.C.

if my reasoning is correct, you may share my conclusions, and exercise some forethought for yourselves at least, if you are actually unwilling to do so for the Hellenes as a whole; but that if you think that I am talking nonsense, and am out of my senses, you may both now and hereafter decline to attend to me as though I were a sane man.

[21] The rise of Philip to greatness from such small and humble beginnings; the mistrustful and quarrelsome attitude of the Hellenes towards one another; the fact that his growth out of what he was into what he is was a far more extraordinary thing than would be his subjugation of all that remains, when he has already secured so much;—all this and all similar themes, upon which I might speak at length, I will pass over. [22] But I see that all men, beginning with yourselves, have conceded to him the very thing which has been at issue in every Hellenic war during the whole of the past. And what is this? It is the right to act as he pleases—to mutilate and to strip the Hellenic peoples, one by one, to attack and to enslave their cities. [23] For seventy-three years you were the leading people of Hellas, and the Spartans for thirty years save one; and in these last times, after the battle of Leuctra, the Thebans too acquired some power: yet neither to you nor to Thebes nor to Sparta was such a right ever conceded by the Hellenes, as the right to do whatever you pleased. Far from it! [24] First of all it was your own behaviour—or rather that of the Athenians of that day— which some thought immoderate; and all, even those who had no grievance against Athens, felt bound to join the injured parties, and to make war upon you. Then, in their turn, the Spartans, when they had acquired an empire and succeeded to a supremacy like your own, attempted to go beyond all bounds and to disturb the established order to an unjustifiable extent;

476–404 B.C.

404–376 B.C.

and once more, all, even those who had no grievance against them, had recourse to war. [25] Why mention the others? For we ourselves and the Spartans, though we could originally allege no injury done by the one people to the other, nevertheless felt bound to go to war on account of the wrongs which we saw the rest suffering. And yet all the offences of the Spartans in those thirty years of power, and of your ancestors in their seventy years, were less, men of Athens, than the wrongs inflicted upon the Greeks by Philip, in the thirteen years, not yet completed, during which he has been to the fore. Less do I say? They are not a fraction of them. [26] [A few words will easily prove this.] I say nothing of Olynthus, and Methone, and Apollonia, and thirty-two cities in the Thracian region, all annihilated by him with such savagery, that a visitor to the spot would find it difficult to tell that they had ever been inhabited. I remain silent in regard to the extirpation of the great Phocian race. But what is the condition of Thessaly? Has he not robbed their very cities of their governments, and set up tetrarchies, that they may be enslaved, not merely by whole cities, but by whole tribes at a time? [27] Are not the cities of Euboea even now ruled by tyrants, and that in an island that is neighbour to Thebes and Athens? Does he not write expressly in his letters, 'I am at peace with those who choose to obey me'? And what he thus writes he does not fail to act upon; for he is gone to invade the Hellespont; he previously went to attack Ambracia; the great city of Elis in the Peloponnese is his; he has recently intrigued against Megara; and neither Hellas nor the world beyond it is large enough to contain the man's ambition. [28] But though all of us, the Hellenes, see and hear these things, we send no representatives to one another to discuss the matter; we show no indignation; we are in so evil a mood, so deep have the lines

Philip's
wrongs

A pro-Macedonian oligarchy established in Elis, circa 344 B.C.

99

been dug which sever city from city, that up to this very day we are unable to act as either our interest or our duty require. [29] We cannot unite; we can form no combination for mutual support or friendship; but we look on while the man grows greater, because every one has made up his mind (as it seems to me) to profit by the time during which his neighbour is being ruined, and no one cares or acts for the safety of the Hellenes. For we all know that Philip is like the recurrence or the attack of a fever or other illness, in his descent upon those who fancy themselves for the present well out of his reach. [30] And further, you must surely realize that all the wrongs that the Hellenes suffered from the Spartans or ourselves they at least suffered at the hands of true-born sons of Hellas; and (one might conceive) it was as though a lawful son, born to a great estate, managed his affairs in some wrong or improper way;— his conduct would in itself deserve blame and denunciation, but at least it could not be said that he was not one of the family, or was not the heir to the property. [31] But had it been a slave or a supposititious son that was thus ruining and spoiling an inheritance to which he had no title, why, good Heavens! how infinitely more scandalous and reprehensible all would have declared it to be. And yet they show no such feeling in regard to Philip, although not only is he no Hellene, not only has he no kinship with Hellenes, but he is not even a barbarian from a country that one could acknowledge with credit;—he is a pestilent Macedonian, from whose country it used not to be possible to buy even a slave of any value.

[32] And in spite of this, is there any degree of insolence to which he does not proceed? Not content with annihilating cities, does he not manage the Pythian games, the common meeting of the Hellenes, and send his slaves to preside over the competition in his absence?

[Is he not master of Thermopylae, and of the passes which lead into Hellenic territory? Does he not hold that district with garrisons and mercenaries? Has he not taken the precedence in consulting the oracle, and thrust aside ourselves and the Thessalians and Dorians and the rest of the Amphictyons, though the right is not one which is given even to all of the Hellenes?] [33] Does he not write to the Thessalians to prescribe the constitution under which they are to live? Does he not send one body of mercenaries to Porthmus, to expel the popular party of Eretria, and another to Oreus, to set up Philistides as tyrant? And yet the Hellenes see these things and endure them, gazing (it seems to me) as they would gaze at a hailstorm—each people praying that it may not come their way, but no one trying to prevent it. Nor is it only his outrages upon Hellas that go unresisted. [34] No one resists even the aggressions which are committed against himself. Ambracia and Leucas belong to the Corinthians—he has attacked them: Naupactus to the Achaeans—he has sworn to hand it over to the Aetolians: Echinus to the Thebans—he has taken it from them, and is now marching against their allies the Byzantines—is it not so? [35] And of our own possessions, to pass by all the rest, is not Cardia, the greatest city in the Chersonese, in his hands? Thus are we treated; and we are all hesitating and torpid, with our eyes upon our neighbours, distrusting one another, rather than the man whose victims we all are. But if he treats us collectively in this outrageous fashion, what do you think he will do, when he has become master of each of us separately?

[36] What then is the cause of these things? For as it was not without reason and just cause that the Hellenes in old days were so prompt for freedom, so it is not without reason or cause that they are now so prompt to be slaves. There was a spirit, men of Athens,

His favored
treatment at
Delphi

His opposi-
tion to
democracies

a spirit in the minds of the people in those days, which is absent to-day—the spirit which vanquished the wealth of Persia, which led Hellas in the path of freedom, and never gave way in face of battle by sea or by land; a spirit whose extinction to-day has brought universal ruin and turned Hellas upside down. What was this spirit? [It was nothing subtle nor clever.] [37] It meant that men who took money from those who aimed at dominion or at the ruin of Hellas were execrated by all; that it was then a very grave thing to be convicted of bribery; that the punishment for the guilty man was the heaviest that could be inflicted; that for him there could be no plea for mercy, nor hope of pardon. [38] No orator, no general, would then sell the critical opportunity whenever it arose—the opportunity so often offered to men by fortune, even when they are careless and their foes are on their guard. They did not barter away the harmony between people and people, nor their own mistrust of the tyrant and the foreigner, nor any of these high sentiments. Where are such sentiments now? [39] They have been sold in the market and are gone; and those have been imported in their stead, through which the nation lies ruined and plague-stricken —the envy of the man who has received his hire; the amusement which accompanies his avowal; [the pardon granted to those whose guilt is proved;] the hatred of one who censures the crime; and all the appurtenances of corruption. [40] For as to ships, numerical strength, unstinting abundance of funds and all other material of war, and all the things by which the strength of cities is estimated, every people can command these in greater plenty and on a larger scale by far than in old days. But all these resources are rendered unserviceable, ineffectual, unprofitable, by those who traffic in them.

[41] That these things are so to-day, you doubtless see, and need no testimony of mine: and that in times

gone by the opposite was true, I will prove to you, not by any words of my own, but by the record inscribed by your ancestors on a pillar of bronze, and placed on the Acropolis [not to be a lesson to themselves—they needed no such record to put them in a right mind—but to be a reminder and an example to you of the zeal that you ought to display in such a cause]. [42] What then is the record? 'Arthmius, son of Pythonax, of Zeleia, is an outlaw, and is the enemy of the Athenian people and their allies, he and his house.' Then follows the reason for which this step was taken—'because he brought the gold from the Medes into the Peloponnese.' [43] Such is the record. Consider, in Heaven's name, what must have been the mind of the Athenians of that day, when they did this, and their conception of their position. They set up a record, that because a man of Zeleia, Arthmius by name, a slave of the King of Persia (for Zeleia is in Asia), as part of his service to the king, had brought gold, not to Athens, but to the Peloponnese, he should be an enemy of Athens and her allies, he and his house, and that they should be outlaws. [44] And this outlawry is no such disfranchisement as we ordinarily mean by the word. For what would it matter to a man of Zeleia, that he might have no share in the public life of Athens? But there is a clause in the Law of Murder, dealing with those in connexion with whose death the law does not allow a prosecution for murder [but the slaying of them is to be a holy act]: 'And let him die an outlaw,' it runs. The meaning, accordingly, is this—that the slayer of such a man is to be pure from all guilt. [45] They thought, therefore, that the safety of all the Hellenes was a matter which concerned themselves—apart from this belief, it could not have mattered to them whether any one bought or corrupted men in the Peloponnese; and whenever they detected such offenders, they carried their punishment and their

The case of
Arthmius of
Zeleia

A decree of
the fifth
century

vengeance so far as to pillory their names for ever. As
the natural consequence, the Hellenes were a terror to
the foreigner, not the foreigner to the Hellenes. It is
not so now. Such is not your attitude in these or in
other matters. But what is it? [46] [You know it yourselves; for why should I accuse you explicitly on every
point? And that of the rest of the Hellenes is like your
own, and no better; and so I say that the present situation demands our utmost earnestness and good counsel.]
And what counsel? Do you bid me tell you, and will you
not be angry if I do so?

[*He reads from the document.*]

[47] Now there is an ingenuous argument, which is
used by those who would reassure the city, to the effect
that, after all, Philip is not yet in the position once
held by the Spartans, who ruled everywhere over sea
and land, with the king for their ally, and nothing to
withstand them; and that, none the less, Athens defended
herself even against them, and was not swept away.
Since that time the progress in every direction, one may
say, has been great, and has made the world to-day
very different from what it was then; but I believe that
in no respect has there been greater progress or development than in the art of war. [48] In the first place,
I am told that in those days the Spartans and all our
other enemies would invade us for four or five months—
during, that is, the actual summer—and would damage
Attica with infantry and citizen-troops, and then return
home again. And so old-fashioned were the men of that
day—nay rather, such true citizens—that no one ever
purchased any object from another for money, but their
warfare was of a legitimate and open kind. [49] But now,
as I am sure you see, most of our losses are the result
of treachery, and no issue is decided by open conflict

The Pelo-
ponnesian
War

or battle; while you are told that it is not because he leads a column of heavy infantry that Philip can march wherever he chooses, but because he has attached to himself a force of light infantry, cavalry, archers, mercenaries, and similar troops. [50] And whenever, with such advantages, he falls upon a State which is disordered within, and in their distrust of one another no one goes out in defence of its territory, he brings up his engines and besieges them. I pass over the fact that summer and winter are alike to him—that there is no close season during which he suspends operations. [51] But if you all know these things and take due account of them, you surely must not let the war pass into Attica, nor be dashed from your seat through looking back to the simplicity of those old hostilities with Sparta. You must guard against him, at the greatest possible distance, both by political measures and by preparations; you must prevent his stirring from home, instead of grappling with him at close quarters in a struggle to the death. [52] For, men of Athens, we have many natural advantages for a war, if we are willing to do our duty. There is the character of his country, much of which we can harry and damage, and a thousand other things. But for a pitched battle he is in better training than we.

[53] Nor have you only to recognize these facts, and to resist him by actual operations of war. You must also by reasoned judgement and of set purpose come to execrate those who address you in his interest, remembering that it is impossible to master the enemies of the city, until you punish those who are serving them in the city itself. [54] And this, before God and every Heavenly Power—this you will not be able to do; for you have reached such a pitch of folly or distraction or—I know not what to call it; for often has the fear actually entered my mind, that some more than mortal power may be driving our fortunes to ruin—that to enjoy their abuse,

or their malice, or their jests, or whatever your motive may chance to be, you call upon men to speak who are hirelings, and some of whom would not even deny it; and you laugh to hear their abuse of others. [55] And terrible as this is, there is yet worse to be told. For you have actually made political life safer for these men, than for those who uphold your own cause. And yet observe what calamities the willingness to listen to such men lays up in store. I will mention facts known to you all.

[56] In Olynthus, among those who were engaged in public affairs, there was one party who were on the side of Philip, and served his interests in everything; and another whose aim was their city's real good, and the preservation of their fellow citizens from bondage. Which were the destroyers of their country? which betrayed the cavalry, through whose betrayal Olynthus perished? Those whose sympathies were with Philip's cause; those who, while the city still existed brought such dishonest and slanderous charges against the speakers whose advice was for the best, that, in the case of Apollonides at least, the people of Olynthus was even induced to banish the accused.

[57] Nor is this instance of the unmixed evil wrought by these practices in the case of the Olynthians an exceptional one, or without parallel elsewhere. For in Eretria, when Plutarchus and the mercenaries had been got rid of, and the people had control of the city and of Porthmus, one party wished to entrust the State to you, the other to entrust it to Philip. And through listening mainly, or rather entirely, to the latter, these poor luckless Eretrians were at last persuaded to banish the advocates of their own interests. [58] For, as you know, Philip, their ally, sent Hipponicus with a thousand mercenaries, stripped Porthmus of its walls, and set up three tyrants—Hipparchus, Automedon, and Cleitarchus;

Treachery in Olynthus, 348 B.C.

Eretria on Euboea turns to Philip

and since then he has already twice expelled them from the country when they wished to recover their position [sending on the first occasion the mercenaries commanded by Eurylochus, on the second, those under Parmenio].

[59] And why go through the mass of the instances? Enough to mention how in Oreus Philip had, as his agents, Philistides, Menippus, Socrates, Thoas, and Agapaeus—the very men who are now in possession of the city—and every one knew the fact; while a certain Euphraeus, who once lived here in Athens, acted in the interests of freedom, to save his country from bondage. [60] To describe the insults and the contumely with which he met would require a long story; but a year before the capture of the town he laid an information of treason against Philistides and his party, having perceived the nature of their plans. A number of men joined forces, with Philip for their paymaster and director, and haled Euphraeus off to prison as a disturber of the peace. [61] Seeing this, the democratic party in Oreus, instead of coming to the rescue of Euphraeus, and beating the other party to death, displayed no anger at all against them, and agreed with a malicious pleasure that Euphraeus deserved his fate. After this the conspirators worked with all the freedom they desired for the capture of the city, and made arrangements for the execution of the scheme; while any of the democratic party, who perceived what was going on, maintained a panic-stricken silence, remembering the fate of Euphraeus. So wretched was their condition, that though this dreadful calamity was confronting them, no one dared open his lips, until all was ready and the enemy was advancing up to the walls. Then the one party set about the defence, the other about the betrayal of the city. [62] And when the city had been captured in this base and shameful manner, the suc-

A similar
fifth column
in Oreus on
Euboea

343 B.C.

cessful party governed despotically: and of those who
had been their own protectors, and had been ready to
treat Euphraeus with all possible harshness, they expelled some and murdered others; while the good Euphraeus killed himself, thus testifying to the righteousness and purity of his motives in opposing Philip on
behalf of his countrymen.

[63] Now for what reason, you may be wondering,
were the peoples of Olynthus and Eretria and Oreus
more agreeably disposed towards Philip's advocates than
towards their own? The reason was the same as it is
with you—that those who speak for your true good can
never, even if they would, speak to win popularity with
you; they are constrained to inquire how the State may
be saved: while their opponents, in the very act of
seeking popularity, are co-operating with Philip. [64]
The one party said, 'You must pay taxes;' the other,
'There is no need to do so.' The one said, 'Go to war,
and do not trust him;' the other, 'Remain at peace,'—
until they were in the toils. And—not to mention each
separately—I believe that the same thing was true of
all. The one side said what would enable them to win
favour; the other, what would secure the safety of their
State. And at last the main body of the people accepted
much that they proposed—not now from any such desire for gratification, nor from ignorance, but as a con-
cession to circumstances, thinking that their cause was
now wholly lost. [65] It is this fate, I solemnly assure
you, that I dread for you, when the time comes that
you make your reckoning, and realize that there is no
longer anything that can be done. May you never find
yourselves, men of Athens, in such a position! Yet in
any case, it were better to die ten thousand deaths, than
to do anything out of servility towards Philip [or to
sacrifice any of those who speak for your good]. A noble
recompense did the people in Oreus receive, for entrust-

ing themselves to Philip's friends, and thrusting Euphraeus aside! [66] and a noble recompense the democracy of Eretria, for driving away your envoys, and surrendering to Cleitarchus! They are slaves, scourged and butchered! A noble clemency did he show to the Olynthians, who elected Lasthenes to command the cavalry, and banished Apollonides! [67] It is folly, and it is cowardice, to cherish hopes like these, to give way to evil counsels, to refuse to do anything that you should do, to listen to the advocates of the enemy's cause, and to fancy that you dwell in so great a city that, whatever happens, you will not suffer any harm. [68] Aye, and it is shameful to exclaim after the event, 'Why, who would have expected this? Of course, we ought to have done, or not to have done, such and such things!' The Olynthians could tell you of many things, to have foreseen which in time would have saved them from destruction. So too could the people of Oreus, and the Phocians, and every other people that has been destroyed. But how does that help them now? [69] So long as the vessel is safe, be it great or small, so long must the sailor and the pilot and every man in his place exert himself and take care that no one may capsize it by design or by accident: but when the seas have overwhelmed it, all their efforts are in vain. So it is, men of Athens, with us. [70] While we are still safe, with our great city, our vast resources, our noble name, what are we to do? Perhaps some one sitting here has long been wishing to ask this question. Aye, and I will answer it, and will move my motion; and you shall carry it, if you wish. We ourselves, in the first place, must conduct the resistance and make preparation for it—with ships, that is, and money, and soldiers. For though all but ourselves give way and become slaves, we at least must contend for freedom. [71] And when we have made all these preparations ourselves, and let them be seen, then let us call

The proposal

upon the other states for aid, and send envoys to carry our message [in all directions—to the Peloponnese, to Rhodes, to Chios, to the king; for it is not unimportant for his interests either that Philip should be prevented from subjugating the world]; that so, if you persuade them, you may have partners to share the danger and the expense, in case of need; and if you do not, you may at least delay the march of events. [72] For since the war is with a single man, and not against the strength of a united state, even delay is not without its value, any more than were those embassies of protest which last year went round the Peloponnese, when I and Polyeuctus, that best of men, and Hegesippus and the other envoys went on our tour, and forced him to halt, so that he neither went to attack Acarnania, nor set out for the Peloponnese. [73] But I do not mean that we should call upon the other states, if we are not willing to take any of the necessary steps ourselves. It is folly to sacrifice what is our own, and then pretend to be anxious for the interests of others—to neglect the present, and alarm others in regard to the future. I do not propose this. I say that we must send money to the forces in the Chersonese, and do all that they ask of us; that we must make preparation ourselves, while we summon, convene, instruct, and warn the rest of the Hellenes. That is the policy for a city with a reputation such as yours. [74] But if you fancy that the people of Chalcis or of Megara will save Hellas, while you run away from the task, you are mistaken. They may well be content if they can each save themselves. The task is yours. It is the prerogative that your forefathers won, and through many a great peril bequeathed to you. [75] But if each of you is to sit and consult his inclinations, looking for some way by which he may escape any personal action, the first consequence will be that you will never find any one who will act; and the second, I fear, that the day

The diplomatic offensive of 342 B.C.

will come when we shall be forced to do, at one and the same time, all the things we wish to avoid.

[76] This then is my proposal, and this I move. If the proposal is carried out, I think that even now the state of our affairs may be remedied. But if any one has a better proposal to make, let him make it, and give us his advice. And I pray to all the gods that whatever be the decision that you are about to make, it may be for your good.

THE LETTER OF PHILIP

INTRODUCTION

Many manuscripts of Demosthenes include a strange document, clearly not by the orator himself, but bearing on the period of which he so often speaks. It is called *The Letter of Philip*. Although scholars have sometimes denied the authenticity of this work, the grounds for skepticism are slight and it seems more likely that it is exactly what it purports to be, a letter written around 340 B.C. by Philip or his chancery, and sent to Athens as a complaint about the recent deterioration of relations between the two states. It concludes with the warning that Macedon will no longer tolerate what it regards as Athens' repeated aggressions.

It presents a substantial and, to those familiar only with Demosthenes, a surprising case against Athens' recent conduct, and in doing so it directly contradicts the *Philippics*. In it Athens appears as a meddler, an inveterate and malicious opponent of Philip, and a dissembler. Philip stresses Macedon's repeated willingness and Athens' consistent refusal to negotiate or arbitrate. The point is a telling one, for despite Clausewitz' dictum that the aggressor, having nothing to lose and all to gain, is often more willing to negotiate than his victim, Athens could produce little proof that she had ever seriously sought a fair settlement with Philip, and, as this letter makes clear, she had pursued what might in Pella seem a policy every bit as aggressive as Philip's seemed in Athens.

The tone of the letter, which I have attempted to bring over in this translation, is light, allusive, at times colloquial, a smooth but translucent surface under which rages Philip's bitterness at Athens. What offends him most is that Athens poses as the embodiment of Hellenism and acts as its antithesis. He sees in recent events the abandonment of the past traditions of Greece (§7), a neglect of her religious conventions (§4) and an unhellenic rejection of common sense most clearly revealed in Athens' toleration of pedantry [§14] and of inconsistency [§9]. To Philip these amount to a most grievous failing: *paranomia,* here tamely and despondently rendered "illegality," but something which is in fact both wider and narrower than the neglect of law. It is the refusal to follow those usually unwritten rules of behavior that set the Greeks apart from other men. Contempt for religion, for reason, and for tradition are its prime manifestations. *The Letter of Philip* is thus simultaneously a reminder of Philip's claim to be a Hellene and a condemnation of Athens for despising her heritage. The scorn, the sarcasm, the offended reasonableness of this letter make it an extraordinary revelation of Philip's attitude, just as its contents provide a rare opportunity to hear another side of the unfortunate events of the 340's.

———

Philip sends greetings to the Athenian council and assembly:

Since you have not responded to the several embassies which I despatched in the hope of preserving our sworn obligations and agreements, I thought it necessary to send you an account of the issues and complaints outstanding between us. Please do not be surprised at the length of this communique, for our disagreements are many and each calls for a precise clarification.

[2] First, the matter of the herald Nicias who was kidnapped from my territory. My objection here is not so much that you refused to punish the wrongdoers, but that you imprisoned the unfortunate man for nine months, and read in public the letters of ours which he was carrying.

Second, the matter of the Thasians who received

Action pro-
hibited by the
Peace of
346 B.C.

in their port triremes of the Byzantines and any pirates
who wished to enter. You paid no attention to this,
though our treaty is explicit in declaring that those who
undertake such actions are to be considered enemies.

Athenian gen-
eral sent to
Thrace in
341 B.C.

[3] Third, at roughly the same time, Diopeithes
made an incursion into my territory, enslaved Crobyle
and Tiristasis, ravaged the neighboring sections of
Thrace, and, not content with these illegalities, seized
my ambassador Amphilochus, who had come to negotiate about the prisoners, tortured him in unspeakable
ways, and then exacted a ransom of nine talents. These
actions won the approval of your assembly. [4] Now to
violate the religious sanctity of a herald or of ambassadors is acknowledged by all men to be a crime, not
least by you Athenians. For example, when the Megareans killed Anthemocritus, the state of Athens went so
far as to exclude them from the Eleusinian mysteries
and to set up a statue before the city gates to serve as
a memorial of their injustice. Is there any way in which
you can justify your present imitation of the very act
for which you came to hate the Megareans?

[5] Furthermore, your general Callias captured all

Euboean poli-
tician, led
revolts in
Euboea,
341 B.C.

the cities in the Pagasean gulf, though they were covered in the treaty you swore and though they were
bound in alliance to me. He sold into slavery everyone
who was travelling to Macedon, just as if he had captured them in war. And for these actions he was
officially commended. I confess I see no difference between this state of affairs and declared war. In our last

Before
346 B.C.

conflict you incited pirates against me, sold travellers
to Macedon, brought aid to my opponents, and did
what you could to hurt my territory.

[6] You have revealed the extent of your illegality

Compare
Philippic III
§71

and hostility by sending ambassadors to the Persian
king in an attempt to induce him to make war on me.
This is a surprising reversal of policy, for before he

took Egypt and Phoenicia you voted that if he made
any trouble, you would summon me and all the other
Greeks to stop him. [7] The vehemence of your feeling
against me now leads you to negotiate an offensive
alliance with him. There was a time, I understand, when
your forefathers condemned the Peisistratids for leading
the king of Persia against the Greeks. But you feel no
shame in doing the very thing for which you kept
condemning the tyrants.

[8] On top of everything else you propose decrees
to warn me to let Teres and Cersobleptes rule Thrace,
"since they are Athenian citizens." I fail to find these
gentlemen listed in the codicil of the peace agreement
or in the inscribed text, nor was I aware that they are
Athenian citizens. I do seem to recollect that Teres
once joined in an expedition of mine against you, and
that when Cersobleptes wanted to swear the oath separately to my ambassadors, he was prohibited by your
generals who called him "an enemy of the Athenian
people." [9] Perhaps you will explain to me how it is
proper and just to call the same man an enemy of the
city when it seems expedient to you, and to assert that
he is a citizen when you want to harass me. And when
Sitalces, your honorary citizen, died, how was it just
for you immediately to become the friend of the man
who killed him, and for Cersobleptes' sake to undertake
a war against us? You know perfectly well that no one
who receives those honorary awards of yours ever
shows the slightest respect for your laws and decrees.
[10] But perhaps you would prefer I pass over all these
matters and speak more succinctly: You gave citizenship
to Euagoras of Cyprus and Dionysius of Syracus and to
their descendants. Persuade the people who drove those
two off their thrones to take them back again and you
may take from me every inch of Thrace that Teres and
Cersobleptes ever ruled. But if while you are making

355 B.C.

490 B.C.

Rulers in
Thrace award-
ed honorary
Athenian
citizenship

Euagoras II
of Cyprus.
Dionysius II
of Syracuse,
ruled 367–
57 B.C.

trouble for me, you are unwilling even to protest to those who overpowered Euagoras and Dionysius, don't you think I have some grounds for protecting my own interests?

[11] I could advance many further arguments on this matter, but I prefer to move on to another topic. I make no secret of my aid to the Cardians. I was, after all, their ally before the peace, and you did not want to arbitrate, despite repeated requests from me and repeated appeals from the Cardians. If I abandoned allies who have always been loyal to me and showed greater consideration to you who have sought out every possible chance to cause me trouble, wouldn't I be the most unreliable man alive?

[12] There is another matter I must call to your attention. You have lately surpassed even your former arrogance in complaining to me about the Cardian affair. Just recently when the Peparethians said they were mistreated you ordered your general to force me to compensate them—and these were men that I punished less than they deserved, since in time of peace they seized Halonnesus and refused to surrender either the garrison or the territory despite my many appeals. [13] You, of course, paid no attention to the Peparethians' mistreatment of me, while noticing every detail of my retaliation. But the fact is that I did not take the island away from them or from you, but from the pirate Sostratus. If you say that you voluntarily handed the island over to Sostratus, you admit you commission pirates. But if you didn't want Sostratus to control it, what does it matter to you if I have taken it over, when I at least have made this area safe for naval traffic? [14] And when I showed such consideration to your city that I offered to give you the island, the politicians wouldn't let you "receive it" but advised you to "receive it back." Thus, if I obeyed your command, I would

Philip defended Cardia in Thrace from Diopeithes, 341 B.C.

The crisis over Halonnesus, 343 B.C.

Compare Aeschines *Against Ctesiphon* §83

admit that I had what was not mine; but if I didn't give up the area, the people would distrust me. I saw through this scheme, and invited you to arbitrate the matter; if it were adjudged mine I would "give" the place to you; if it were adjudged yours, then I would "give it back" to the state. [15] Though I suggested this a number of times, you were not interested. The Peparethians, however, seized the island. What do you think I should have done? Should I have failed to take action against violators of the treaty? Should I have failed to punish an open insult? And further, if the island really belonged to the Peparethians, what business of yours was it to demand it back? But if the island was yours, why weren't you angry at *them,* since they were the ones who took what was not theirs.

[16] Our relations have so deteriorated that when I wanted to cross over to the Hellespont by ship, I was forced to send my army to secure the coast line. Your colonists, as authorized by Polycrates' decree, made war on us. Your enactments encouraged them. Your general invited the Byzantines to join him and quite openly announced that you had told him to make war if he had the chance. Under this provocation I nonetheless took no action against your city, your ships, or your territory, though I was strong enough to seize most or all of these. Instead I kept inviting you to arbitrate our mutual disputes. [17] Which do you think is more honourable: to settle our disputes by negotiations or by arms? to be referee yourself or to persuade someone else to be? Bear in mind how anomalous it is for you to compel the Thasians and the Maronites to arbitrate while you will not use the same method to settle your own disputes with me. Your reluctance is all the more strange because you know perfectly well that even if you lose the case, you risk nothing, while if you win, you will gain territory now under our control.

Circa 341 B.C.

Athens forces
towns in
Thrace to
arbitrate

[18] But this seems the strangest thing of all: when I chose ambassadors from the whole league with the thought that they would also be witnesses, and sent them to you, you would not even listen to their proposals, even though I wanted to arrange with you a just settlement on behalf of the Greeks. You turned down a perfect opportunity either to reassure those who feared we would make some trouble for them or clearly to show me up as the most unreliable man alive. [19] These proposals of mine contributed to the state's interests but not to the orators' pocketbooks. People who know your system of government say that for them peace is war and war is peace. There is always money to be made from the generals either by supporting them, or by harassing them. And in addition by publicly slandering the most distinguished citizens and the most famous world figures the orators can convince the people that they are the loyalest democrats.

[20] A small expenditure on my part would easily stop their character assassination, and make them my enthusiastic supporters. But I will not stoop to buying good relations with you from men who add this final touch of bravado to all their other offences—they are trying to stir up a dispute between us over a place to which I think I have a far stronger title than any other claimant, Amphipolis. [21] For if it belongs to those who originally controlled it, isn't it ours, since our ancestor Alexander first possessed the place? (He was the one who set up the gold statue in Delphi as an offering for all the Medes he captured.) But if someone should dispute this title and contend that it belongs to those who controlled it later, my claim is still strong. I expelled the men who had driven you out and who had been settled there by the Spartans, and I took the place myself. [22] Now we all live in cities that were either founded by our forefathers or won in war. You are seek-

Athens' refusal to negotiate

Philip's claim to Amphipolis

Circa 479 B.C.

ing a city which you neither had originally nor control now. You lasted only the shortest time in that area, and yourself provide strong evidence for my case. My despatches frequently touched on that city and you acknowledged that we had legal claim to it, both when you made peace with me while I held it, and then when you made an alliance on the same terms. [23] I find it hard to imagine a more secure title than one that in the first place we inherited from our forefathers, in the second place was confirmed by war, and lastly conceded by you who are notoriously prone to go to law over matters that are none of your business.

These then are my complaints. Since you have taken the initiative and, thanks to my restraint, now interfere even more menacingly in my affairs, and since you are doing all you can to make trouble, with justice on my side I will defend myself; with the gods as witnesses I will give my opposition to you my most studied attention.

THE DEBATE ON THE CROWN
From the
AGAINST CTESIPHON OF AESCHINES

INTRODUCTION

The Letter of Philip ended with an intentional ambiguity. The last paragraph is a clear enough warning that Philip will not tolerate Athens' meddling, but the final phrase is something short of an outright declaration of war. The deliberately vague "I will give my opposition to you my most studied attention" threatened without quite closing the door on negotiation. But whatever hope of settlement still existed in mid-summer 340 B.C. soon disappeared. Later the same summer Philip moved against Byzantium and war began again.

It was, however, a dispute in the Delphic Amphictyony that brought the war into central Greece. The meeting of the sacred delegates in the spring of 339 B.C. consisted of a series of power plays the best narrative of which is in Aeschines' speech *Against Ctesiphon,* §§115-29. The outcome was a vote against the Amphissian Locrians, and it seemed a victory for Athens. The military operations that resulted from this vote, however, required a strong leader. The obvious candidate was Philip and in 338 B.C. the obvious invitation was extended to him. As soon as he moved his army into north central Greece, he seized Elateia, a Phocian town that secured his communications but also put him in a position to march on Thebes or Athens.

When the news of the capture of Elateia reached Athens, the city was in consternation until the confident rhetoric of Demosthenes, so proudly described in *On the Crown* §§168–79, convinced the people to ally with Thebes and prepare to march against Philip. Whatever Philip's intentions when he seized Elateia, the combination of Athens and Thebes against him left little alternative. The battle was joined at Chaeronea in Boeotia on 2 August 338 B.C. Demosthenes, who served as a hoplite in the Athenian force, escaped the fate of so many of his comrades and returned to Athens where under the moderate peace arrangements made with Philip he continued to exercise considerable political power.

He was not, however, unchallenged. In 330 B.C. an old opponent, Aeschines, renewed his long-standing indictment of one Ctesiphon who six years earlier had proposed honoring Demosthenes with a gold crown for his services to the state. Although on the surface such an accusation might seem an admirable attempt to preserve constitutional niceties, even the slightest familiarity with Athenian politics made it clear that it was an attack on Demosthenes. Naturally Demosthenes served as advocate for Ctesiphon.

The two principal speeches of the trial are preserved: one is Aeschines' oration *Against Ctesiphon,* the other is Demosthenes' address entitled *On the Crown.* No where in Attic oratory is there a more elaborate or empassioned exchange. When the speeches are set side by side, they provide one of the best sources of information about the whole period of the rise of Philip and one of the best opportunities to see Attic rhetoric in action and to appreciate the emotion of Athenian political life.

The technical charges against Ctesiphon were two: First that he had proposed that Demosthenes be honored *before* the orator had gone through his formal audit at the end of his term of office; second that he had specified that the crown be proclaimed *in the theatre.* In both respects Ctesiphon probably violated the letter of Athenian law, though proclaiming such an award in the theatre had at least ample precedent. But an Athenian jury was not likely to be distracted by what it would consider pedantic technicalities. The issue was whether or not they would condemn Demosthenes for his past policies; everyone in the court knew this. Thus the two speakers pass over these legal details rather quickly and concentrate on a third point, Demosthenes' career, his contributions to Athens and his personal life. The following excerpts from C. D. Adams' translation of the *Against Ctesiphon* omit most of the arguments on the two technical issues but reproduce representative portions of the attack on Demosthenes' political and personal behavior.

The opening sections of Aeschines' speech are devoted largely to the exposition of two of his three main theses:

(1) That Ctesiphon's motion is illegal because the law explicitly forbids crowning men before they have gone through their final accounting at the end of their term of office. Demosthenes, Aeschines points out, was still in office when crowned.

(2) That Ctesiphon's motion is illegal because the law specifies that crowns be proclaimed in the senate or in the assembly "but nowhere else." Yet Demosthenes was proclaimed in the theatre.

Aeschines then turns to his third, and most important, thesis, that Demosthenes did not deserve the crown:

[49] But that part of my accusation remains upon which I lay greatest stress: the pretext upon which he claims that the crown is deserved. It reads thus in his motion: "And the herald shall proclaim in the theatre in the presence of the Hellenes that the Athenian people crown him for his merit and uprightness," and that monstrous assertion, "because he continually speaks and does what is best for the people." [50] You see how entirely simple the remainder of our argument becomes, and how easy for you, my hearers, to weigh. For it is obviously incumbent upon me, the complainant, to show this to you, that the praise given to Demosthenes is

false, and that he never began to "speak what was best," nor now "continues to do what is good for the people." If I show this, then Ctesiphon will doubtless lose his case, and justly; for all the laws forbid inserting falsehoods in the decrees of the people. But the defence must show the opposite of this. And you are to be the judges of our pleas.

> After a few comments about Demosthenes' personal life Aeschines outlines the course he will follow in the rest of the speech. He will divide Demosthenes' career into four periods—the first down to the Peace of Philocrates in 346 B.C.; the second the period during which the Peace lasted; the third, the time of the new war with Philip which ended in the battle of Chaeronea (338 B.C.); and finally, the events from Chaeronea to the delivery of the speech. He begins the discussion of the first period with the charge that Demosthenes served the interests of Philip, not of Athens, in the peace negotiations of 346 B.C.

[58] You could have made that former peace, fellow citizens, supported by the joint action of a congress of the Greek states, if certain men had allowed you to wait for the return of the embassies which at that crisis you had sent out among the Greeks, with the call to join you against Philip; and in the course of time the Greeks would of their own accord have accepted your hegemony again. Of this you were deprived, thanks to Demosthenes and Philocrates, and the bribes which they took in their conspiracy against the common weal.

Period One: §§58–78

Athens might have made peace in 346 B.C. at the head of a Hellenic alliance

[59] But if such a statement as I have just made, falling suddenly on your ears, is too incredible to some of you, permit me to suggest how you ought to listen to the rest of my argument: When we take our seats to audit the accounts of expenditures which extend back a long time, it doubtless sometimes happens that we come

from home with a false impression; nevertheless, when the accounts have been balanced, no man is so stubborn as to refuse, before he leaves the room, to assent to that conclusion, whatever it may be, which the figures themselves establish. I ask you to give a similar hearing now. . . .

[62] Philocrates made a motion that we permit Philip to send to us a herald and ambassadors to treat concerning peace. This motion was attacked in the courts as illegal. The time of the trial came. Lycinus, who had indicted him, spoke for the prosecution; Philocrates made answer for himself, and Demosthenes spoke in his behalf; Philocrates was cleared. After this came the archonship of Themistocles. Now Demosthenes came in as senator, not drawn by the lot either as a member of the senate or as a substitute, but through intrigue and bribery; the purpose of it was to enable him to support Philocrates in every way, by word and deed, as the event itself made evident. [63] For now Philocrates carries a second resolution, providing for the election of ten ambassadors, who shall go to Philip and ask him to send hither plenipotentiaries to negotiate peace. Of these ambassadors one was Demosthenes. On his return, Demosthenes was a eulogist of the peace, he agreed with the other ambassadors in their report, and he alone of the senators moved to give safe-conduct to Philip's herald and ambassadors; and in this motion he was in accord with Philocrates, for the one had given permission to send a herald and ambassadors hither, the other gave safe-conduct to the embassy.

[64] As to what followed, I beg you now to pay especial attention. For negotiations were entered into—not with the other ambassadors, who were slandered again and again by Demosthenes after he had changed face, but with Philocrates and Demosthenes (naturally,

Abacus image

348–47 B.C.

347–46 B.C.

Compare
Demosthenes
On the Crown
§§21–24

for they were at once ambassadors and authors of the motions)—first, that you should not wait for the ambassadors whom you had sent out with your summons against Philip, for they wished you to make the peace, not together with the Greeks, but by yourselves; [65] secondly, that you should vote, not only for peace, but also for alliance with Philip, in order that any states which were taking note of what the Athenian democracy was doing might fall into utter discouragement on seeing that, while you were summoning them to war, you had at home voted to make both peace and an alliance; and thirdly, that Cersobleptes, king of Thrace, should not be included in the oaths, nor share the alliance and peace—indeed, an expedition was already being levied against him. [66] Now the man who was buying such services was doing no wrong, for before the oaths had been taken and the agreements entered into, he could not be blamed for negotiating to his own advantage; but the men who sold, who admitted Philip into partnership in the control of the strongholds of the state, were deserving of your great indignation. For the man who now shouts, "Down with Alexander!" and in those days, "Down with Philip!" the man who throws in my face the friendship of Alexander, this man Demosthenes, stole away the opportunities of the city by making the motion that [67] the prytanes call an assembly for the eighth day of Elaphebolion, the day of the sacrifice to Asclepius, and the introductory day of the festival—the sacred day!—a thing that no man remembers ever to have been done before. And what was his pretext? "In order," he says, "that if Philip's ambassadors shall by that time have arrived, the people may most speedily deliberate on their relations with Philip." He thus appropriates the assembly for the ambassadors in advance, before their arrival, cutting short your time, and hurrying on the whole business; and this was in order that

Compare
Demosthenes
On the Crown
§22

Philip

E.g., Demosthenes

The opening
of the
Dionysia, 5
April 346 B.C.

you might make the peace, not in cooperation with the other Greeks, on the return of your ambassadors, but alone.

[68] After this, fellow citizens, Philip's ambassadors arrived; but yours were absent, summoning the Greeks against Philip. Thereupon Demosthenes carries another resolution, in which he provides that we take counsel, not only regarding peace, but on the subject of an alliance also; and that we should do this without waiting for your ambassadors to return, but immediately after the City Dionysia, on the 18th and 19th of the month. As proof of the truth of what I say, hear the resolutions.

Compare
Demosthenes
On the Crown
§28

Resolutions

Athens' allies
pass a synod-
ical resolu-
tion

[69] When now, fellow citizens, the Dionysia were past and the assemblies took place, in the first assembly a resolution of the synod of the allies was read, the substance of which I will give briefly before having it read to you. First, they provided only that you should take counsel regarding peace, and omitted the word "alliance"—and that not inadvertently, but because they looked upon even the peace as necessary, rather than honourable; secondly, they met Demosthenes' bribery with a well-chosen remedy, [70] by adding in their resolution that any Greek state that wished should be permitted within the space of three months to have its name inscribed with the Athenians on the same stone, and to share the oaths and agreements. In this way they were taking two precautions, and those of the greatest importance; for first, they provided the period of three months, a sufficient time for the ambassadors of the Greek states to arrive; and secondly, they sought to secure to the city the good-will of the Greeks, by the provision for a general congress, in order that in case the agreements should be violated, we might not enter

upon the war unprepared and alone—the misfortune that actually came upon us, thanks to Demosthenes. Now that what I say is true, you shall learn by hearing the resolution itself.

The Resolution of the Allies

[71] I acknowledge that I supported this resolution, as did all who spoke in the first of the two assemblies; and the people left the assembly with substantially this supposition, that peace would be made (that, however, it was better not to discuss an alliance, because of our summons to the Greeks), and that the peace would be shared by all the Greeks. Night intervened. We came the next day to the assembly. Then it was that Demosthenes, hastening to get possession of the platform, and leaving no other man an opportunity to speak, said that the propositions of yesterday were utterly useless unless Philip's ambassadors could be persuaded to assent to them. He further said that he could not conceive of peace without alliance. [72] For he said we must not— I remember the expression he used, for the word was as odious as the man—he said we must not "rip off" the alliance from the peace, nor wait for the slow decisions of the other Greeks, but we must either fight ourselves, or by ourselves make the peace. And finally he called Antipater to the platform, and proceeded to ask him a certain question—he had previously told him what he was going to ask, and had instructed him what he was to answer, to the injury of the state. Finally this thing prevailed, Demosthenes forcing you to it by his talk, and Philocrates moving the resolution. [73] One thing remained now for them to do—to betray Cersobleptes and the Thracian coast. This they accomplished on the 25th of Elaphebolion, before Demosthenes set out on the second embassy, the embassy for the ratification of

Demosthenes favors alliance with Philip

One of Philip's ambassadors

the oaths (for this orator of ours, this man who shouts "Down with Alexander!" and "Down with Philip!" has twice been an ambassador to Macedonia, when he need not have gone once—the man who now bids you spit on the Macedonians). Presiding over the assembly on the 25th, for he had gained a seat in the senate by intrigue, he, with the help of Philocrates, betrayed Cersobleptes; [74] for Philocrates unobserved slipped this clause in among the provisions of his resolution, and Demosthenes put it to the vote, that "The members of the synod of the allies do on this day give their oaths to the ambassadors from Philip." But no representative of Cersobleptes had a seat in the synod; and so in providing that those who were sitting in the synod should give oath, he excluded Cersobleptes from the oaths, for he had no place in the synod. [75] As proof that I am speaking the truth, read, if you please, who it was that made this motion, and who it was that put it to vote.

Thrace betrayed

The Resolution

An excellent thing, fellow citizens, an excellent thing is the preservation of the public acts. For the record remains undisturbed, and does not shift sides with political turncoats, but whenever the people desire, it gives them opportunity to discern who have been rascals of old, but have now changed face and claim to be honourable men.

[76] It remains for me to describe his flattery. For Demosthenes, fellow citizens, was senator for a year, yet he will be found never to have invited any other embassy to the seat of honour—nay, that was the first and the only time; and he placed cushions and spread rugs; and at daybreak he came escorting the ambassadors into the theatre, so that he was actually hissed for his unseemly flattery. And when they set out on their return

journey, he hired for them three span of mules, and escorted the ambassadors as far as Thebes, making the city ridiculous. But that I may not wander from my subject, please take the resolution concerning the seats of honour.

Resolution

[77] Now this man it was, fellow citizens, this past master of flattery, who, when informed through scouts of Charidemus that Philip was dead, before any one else had received the news, made up a vision for himself and lied about the gods, pretending that he had received the news, not from Charidemus, but from Zeus and Athena, the gods by whose name he perjures himself by day, and who then converse with him in the night, as he says, and tell him of things to come. And though it was but the seventh day after the death of his daughter, and though the ceremonies of mourning were not yet completed, he put a garland on his head and white raiment on his body, and there he stood making thank-offerings, violating all decency—miserable man, who had lost the first and only one who ever called him "father"! [78] Not that I reproach him for his misfortune, but I am probing his character. For the man who hates his child and is a bad father could never become a safe guide to the people; the man who does not cherish the persons who are nearest and dearest to him, will never care much about you, who are not his kinsmen; the man who is wicked in his private relations would never be found trustworthy in public affairs; and the man who is base at home was never a good and honourable man in Macedonia, for by his journey he changed his position, not his disposition.

[79] Now how it was that he came to reverse his policies (for this is the second period), and what is the

A mercenary general employed by Athens

Period Two: §§79–105

129

reason that policies identical with those of Demosthenes
led to the impeachment and exile of Philocrates, while
Demosthenes suddenly stood forth as accuser of the rest,
and how it is that the pestilential fellow has plunged you
into misfortune, this you ought now especially to hear.

346 B.C.

[80] For as soon as Philip had come this side Thermopylae, and contrary to all expectation had destroyed the
cities of Phocis, and strengthened the Thebans beyond

Compare
Demosthenes'
On the Crown
§35

what was seasonable and advantageous for you, as you
then thought, and when you in alarm had brought in
your movable property from the country districts, and
the ambassadors who had negotiated the peace were
under the gravest accusation—Philocrates and Demosthenes far beyond all the rest, because they not only had
been ambassadors, but were also the authors [81] of
the resolutions, and when it happened at the same time
that Demosthenes and Philocrates had a falling out—
you were able to guess the reasons without much difficulty—when all this disturbance had arisen, then Demosthenes proceeded to take counsel as to his future
course, consulting his own innate corruption, his cowardice, and his jealousy of Philocrates' bribes; and he came
to the conclusion that if he should step forward as the
accuser of his colleagues on the embassy and of Philip,
Philocrates would surely be ruined, his other colleagues
would be put in jeopardy, and he himself would gain
favour, and—scoundrel and traitor to his friends—would
appear to be a faithful servant of the people.

[82] Now when the men who are always the foes
of public tranquillity caught sight of him, they were
delighted, and repeatedly called him to the platform,

Demosthenes'
complaints
about trivial
issues; com-
pare *On the
Crown* §70

and named him our sole and only incorruptible citizen;
and he as often came forward and furnished them
with the sources of disturbance and war. He it is,
fellow citizens, who first discovered Serrhium-Teichus
and Doriscus and Ergisca and Myrtisca and Ganus and

Ganias; for before that we did not even know the names of these places. And he put such forced and perverse interpretation upon what was done, that, if Philip did not send ambassadors, Demosthenes said that Philip was treating the city with contempt; and if he did send them, that he was sending spies, not ambassadors; [83] and if Philip was willing to refer our differences to some state as an equal and impartial arbiter, he said that between Philip and us there was no impartial arbiter. Philip offered to give us Halonnesus; Demosthenes forbade us to accept it if he "gave it," instead of "giving it back," quarrelling over syllables.

Compare *Letter of Philip* §14

An excursus on Athenian relations with Euboea leads up to a further attack on Demosthenes' integrity. Aeschines emphasizes the long standing grievances between Athens and the neighboring island. Demosthenes, he points out, supported a special alliance in 341 B.C. which exempted the Euboeans from the taxes and obligations undertaken by members of Athens' naval league. He alleges that Demosthenes was bribed to betray Athens' best interests. He then moves on to slightly later events:

[106] I come now to the third period, or rather to that bitterest period of all, in which Demosthenes brought ruin upon our state and upon all Hellas by his impiety toward the shrine at Delphi, and by moving the alliance with Thebes—an unjust alliance and utterly unequal. But I will begin with his sins against the gods.

Period Three: §§106–58

[107] There is, fellow citizens, a plain, called the plain of Cirrha, and a harbour, now known as "dedicate and accursed." This district was once inhabited by the Cirrhaeans and the Cragalidae, most lawless tribes, who repeatedly committed sacrilege against the shrine at Delphi and the votive offerings there, and who transgressed against the Amphictyons also. This conduct ex-

Background to the Amphictyonic dispute of 339–38 B.C.

asperated all the Amphictyons, and your ancestors most of all, it is said, and they sought at the shrine of the god an oracle to tell them with what penalty they should visit these men. [108] The Pythia replied that they must fight against the Cirrhaeans and the Cragalidae day and night, utterly ravage their country, enslave the inhabitants, and dedicate the land to the Pythian Apollo and Artemis and Leto and Athena Pronaea, that for the future it lie entirely uncultivated; that they must not till this land themselves nor permit another.

Circa
594 B.C.

Now when they had received this oracle, the Amphictyons voted, on motion of Solon of Athens, a man able as a law-giver and versed in poetry and philosophy, to march against the accursed men according to the oracle of the god. [109] Collecting a great force of the Amphictyons, they enslaved the men, destroyed their harbour and city, and dedicated their land, as the oracle had commanded. Moreover they swore a mighty oath, that they would not themselves till the sacred land nor let another till it, but that they would go to the aid of the god and the sacred land with hand and foot and voice, and all their might. [110] They were not content with taking this oath, but they added an imprecation and a mighty curse concerning this; for it stands thus

The curse

written in the curse: "If any one should violate this," it says, "whether city or private man, or tribe, let them be under the curse," it says, "of Apollo and Artemis and Leto and Athena Pronaea." [111] The curse goes on: That their land bear no fruit; that their wives bear children not like those who begat them, but monsters; that their flocks yield not their natural increase; that defeat await them in camp and court and market-place, and that they perish utterly, themselves, their houses, their whole race; "And never," it says, "may they offer pure sacrifice unto Apollo, nor to Artemis, nor to Leto, nor to Athena Pronaea, and may the gods refuse to accept their offerings." [112] As a proof of this, let the oracle of the god be read; hear the curse; call to mind the oaths that your fathers swore together with all the other Amphictyons.

The Oracle
The Oaths. The Curse

[113] This curse, these oaths, and this oracle stand recorded to this day; yet the Locrians of Amphissa, or rather their leaders, most lawless of men, did till the plain, and they rebuilt the walls of the harbour that was dedicate and accursed, and settled there and collected port-dues from those who sailed into the harbour; and of the deputies who came to Delphi they corrupted some with money, one of whom was Demosthenes. [114] For after he had been elected your deputy, he received two thousand drachmas from the Amphissians, in return for which he was to see that no mention of them should be made in the assembly of the Amphictyons. And it was agreed with him that thereafter twenty minas of the accursed and abominable money should be sent to Athens to him yearly, on condition that he at Athens aid the Amphissians in every way. In consequence of this it has come to pass even more than before, that whatsoever he touches, be it private citizen, or ruler, or democratic state, becomes entangled, every one, in irreparable misfortune.

Demosthenes, Amphictyonic deputy, 343 B.C.

[115] Now behold how providence and fortune triumphed over the impiety of the Amphissians. It was in the archonship of Theophrastus; Diognetus of Anaphlystus was our hieromnemon; as pylagori you elected Meidias of Anagyrus, whom you all remember—I wish for many reasons he were still living—and Thrasycles of Oeum; I was the third. But it happened that we were

The deputies of spring 339 B.C.

Attacked by Demosthenes in Against Meidias

no sooner come to Delphi than Diognetus, the hierom
nemon, fell sick with fever; the same misfortune had
befallen Meidias already. The other Amphictyons tool
their seats. [116] Now it was reported to us by one and
another who wished to show friendship to our city, tha
the Amphissians, who were at that time dominated by
the Thebans and were their abject servants, were in the
act of bringing in a resolution against our city, to the
effect that the people of Athens be fined fifty talents
because we had affixed gilded shields to the new temple
and dedicated them before the temple had been con
secrated, and had written the appropriate inscription
"The Athenians, from the Medes and Thebans when they
fought against Hellas."

The hieromnemon sent for me and asked me to go
into the council and speak to the Amphictyons in behal
of our city—indeed I had already determined of mysel
so to do. [117] When I had entered the council, perhap
a little too impetuously—the other pylagori had with
drawn—and when I was just beginning to speak, one o
the Amphissians, a scurrilous fellow, and, as I plainl
saw, a man of no education whatever, but perhaps also
led on to folly by some divine visitation, cried out, "C
Greeks, if you were in your right mind, you would no
have so much as named the name of the people o
Athens in these sacred days, but you would have de
barred them from the shrine, as men polluted." [118
And at the same time he reminded them of your alliance
with the Phocians, proposed by that man whom we used
to call "Top-knot"; and he went through a long list o
vexatious charges against our city, which angered me
almost beyond endurance as I listened to them then, and
which it is no pleasure to recall now. For as I listened,
was exasperated as never before in my life.

I will pass over the rest of what I said, but thi
occurred to me, to call attention to the impiety of the

Compare De-
mosthenes *On
the Crown*
§§148–51

Trophies from
the battle of
Plataea
479 B.C.

Hegesippus

134

Amphissians in relation to the sacred land; and from the very spot where I was standing I pointed it out to the Amphictyons; for the plain of Cirrha lies just below the shrine and is clearly visible. [119] "You see," I said, "O Amphictyons, the plain yonder tilled by the Amphissians, and pottery works and farm buildings erected there. You see with your own eyes the dedicated and accursed harbour walled again. You know of your own knowledge, and have no need of other witness, how these men have farmed out port-dues, and how they are making money from the sacred harbour." At the same time I called for the reading of the oracle of the god, the oath of our fathers, and the curse that was proclaimed. And I made this declaration: [120] "I, in behalf of the people of Athens, in my own behalf, and in behalf of my children and my house, do come to the help of the god and the sacred land according unto the oath, with hand and foot and voice, and all my powers; and I purge our city of this impiety. As for you, now make your own decision. The sacred baskets are prepared; the sacrificial victims stand ready at the altars; and you are about to pray to the gods for blessings on state and hearth. [121] Consider then with what voice, with what spirit, with what countenance, possessed of what effrontery, you will make your supplications, if you let go unpunished these men, who stand under the ban of the curse. For not in riddles, but plainly is written the penalty to be suffered by those who have been guilty of impiety, and for those who have permitted it; and the curse closes with these words: 'May they who fail to punish them never offer pure sacrifice unto Apollo, nor to Artemis, nor to Leto, nor to Athena Pronaea, and may the gods refuse to accept their offerings.'"

[122] These words I spoke, and many more. And when now I had finished and gone out from the council, there was great outcry and excitement among the Am-

"Punish the Amphissian Locrians!"

§111

phictyons, and nothing more was said about the shields that we had dedicated, but from now on the subject was the punishment of the Amphissians. As it was already late in the day, the herald came forward and made proclamation that all the men of Delphi who were of full age, slaves and free men alike, should come at daybreak on the morrow with shovels and mattocks to the place that is there called the Thyteion. And again the same herald proclaimed that all the hieromnemons and the pylagori should come to the same place to the aid of the god and the sacred land; "And whatever city shall fail to appear, shall be debarred from the shrine and shall be impure and under the curse."

[123] The next morning we came to the designated spot, and descended to the Cirrhaean plain. And when we had despoiled the harbour and burned down the houses, we set out to return. But meanwhile the Locrians of Amphissa, who lived sixty stadia from Delphi, came against us, armed and in full force; and it was only by running that we barely got back to Delphi in safety, for we were in peril of our lives.

Compare
Demosthenes
On the Crown
§151

[124] Now on the next day Cottyphus, the presiding officer, called an "assembly" of the Amphictyons (they call it an "assembly" when not only the pylagori and hieromnemons are called together, but with them those who are sacrificing and consulting the god). Then immediately one charge after another was brought against the Amphissians, and our city was much praised. As the outcome of all that was said, they voted that before the next Pylaea the hieromnemons should assemble at Thermopylae at a time designated, bringing with them a resolution for the punishment of the Amphissians for their sins against the god and the sacred land and the Amphictyons. As proof of what I say, the clerk shall read the decree to you.

A special
session of the
deputies
called

[125] Now when we had reported this decree to our senate, and then to the assembly, and when the people had approved our acts, and the whole city was ready to chose the righteous course, and when Demosthenes had spoken in opposition—he was earning his retaining-fee from Amphissa—and when I had clearly convicted him in your presence, thereupon the fellow, unable to frustrate the city by open means, goes into the senate chamber, expels all listeners, and from the secret session brings out a bill to the assembly, taking advantage of the inexperience of the man who made the motion. [126] And he managed to have this same bill put to vote in the assembly and passed by the people, at the moment when the assembly was on the point of adjourning, when I had already left the place— for I would never have allowed it—and when most of the people had dispersed. Now the substance of the bill was this: "The hieromnemon of the Athenians," it says, "and the pylagori who are at the time in office, shall go to Thermopylae and Delphi at the times appointed by our fathers"; fine in sound, shameful in fact; for it prevents attendance on the special meeting at Thermopylae, which had to be held before the date of the regular meeting. [127] Again in the same decree he writes much more explicity and malignantly: "The hieromnemon of the Athenians," he says, "and the pylagori who are at the time in office, shall take no part with those assembled there, in word or deed or decree, or in any act whatsoever." But what does it mean to "take no part"? Shall I tell you the truth, or what is most agreeable for your ears? I will tell you the truth, for it is the universal habit of speaking to please you that has brought the city to such a pass. It means that you are forbidden to remem-

Back at Athens

339 B.C.

ber the oaths which our fathers swore, or the curse, or the oracle of the god.

[128] And so, fellow citizens, we stayed at home because of this decree, while the other Amphictyons assembled at Thermopylae—all but one city, whose name I would not mention; I pray that misfortune like unto hers may come upon no city of Hellas. And when they were assembled they voted to march against the Amphissians. As general they chose Cottyphus of Pharsalus, who was at the time president of the Amphictyons. Philip was not in Macedonia at that time, nor in Hellas, but in Scythia—so far away as that! And yet presently Demosthenes will dare to say that it was I who brought him against Hellas! [129] Now when they had come through the pass in the first expedition, they dealt very leniently with the Amphissians, for as penalty for their monstrous crimes, they laid a money fine upon them, and ordered them to pay it at the temple within a stated time; and they removed the wicked men who were responsible for what had been done, and restored others, whose piety had forced them into exile. But when the Amphissians failed to pay the money to the god, and had restored the guilty men, and banished those righteous men who had been restored by the Amphictyons, under these circumstances at last the second campaign was made, a long time afterward, when Philip had now returned from his Scythian expedition. It was to us that the gods had offered the leadership in the deed of piety, but Demosthenes' taking of bribes had prevented us.

[130] But did not the gods forewarn us, did they not admonish us, to be on our guard, all but speaking with human voice? No city have I ever seen offered more constant protection by the gods, but more inevitably ruined by certain of its politicians. Was not that portent sufficient which appeared at the Mysteries—the death of the celebrants? In view of this did not Ameiniades

Thebes

Compare Demosthenes On the Crown §148

Compare Demosthenes On the Crown §152

warn you to be on your guard, and to send messengers to Delphi to inquire of the god what was to be done? And did not Demosthenes oppose, and say that the Pythia had gone over to Philip? Boor that he was, gorged with his feast of indulgence from you! [131] And did he not at last from smouldering and ill-omened sacrifices send forth our troops into manifest danger? And yet it was but yesterday that he dared to assert that the reason why Philip did not advance against our country was that the omens were not favourable to him. What punishment, then, do you deserve, you curse of Hellas! For if the conqueror refrained from entering the land of the conquered because the omens were not favourable to him, whereas you, ignorant of the future, sent out our troops before the omens were propitious, ought you to be receiving a crown for the misfortunes of the city, or to have been thrust already beyond her borders?

Philip's conduct after Chaeronea, 338 B.C.

[132] Wherefore what is there, strange and unexpected, that has not happened in our time! For it is not the life of men we have lived, but we were born to be a tale of wonder to posterity. Is not the king of the Persians —he who channelled Athos, he who bridged the Hellespont, he who demanded earth and water of the Greeks, he who dared to write in his letters that he was lord of all men from the rising of the sun unto its setting—is he not struggling now, no longer for lordship over others, but already for his life? And do we not see this glory and the leadership against the Persians bestowed on the same men who liberated the temple of Delphi? [133] But Thebes! Thebes, our neighbour, has in one day been swept from the midst of Hellas—even though justly, for her main policy was wrong, yet possessed by an infatuate blindness and folly that were not of men, but a divine visitation. And the wretched Lacedaemonians, who barely touched these acts at their beginning in connection with the seizure of the temple, they who once

Thebes destroyed, 335 B.C.

Sparta supported Phocis in the Sacred War of 356 B.C.

139

claimed the right to lead the Greeks, are now about to be sent to Alexander to serve as hostages, and to make an exhibition of their misfortunes—destined, themselves and their country, to suffer whatever may please him; their fate dependent on the mercy of the man who has conquered them after receiving unprovoked injury at their hands.

> Aeschines is now prepared to deal with a difficult task—to refute Demosthenes' boast (compare *On the Crown* §188, for example) that he had achieved a diplomatic coup in making the 338 alliance with Thebes. The real cause of this alliance, says Aeschines, was not Demosthenes' diplomatic and oratorical skill, but the change in circumstances and the clear menace of Philip:

Philip moves into Greece, spring 338 B.C.

[140] when finally he had seized Elateia and fortified and garrisoned it, then, and not till then, it was, when the peril was laying hold on them, that they sent for the Athenians. You went out and were on the point of marching into Thebes under arms, horse and foot, before ever Demosthenes had moved one single syllable about an alliance. [141] What brought you into Thebes was the crisis and fear and need of alliance, not Demosthenes.

Compare Demosthenes *On the Crown* §§168–73

For in this whole affair Demosthenes is responsible to you for three most serious mistakes. The first was this: when Philip was nominally making war against you, but really was far more the enemy of Thebes, as the event itself has proved (why need I say more?), Demosthenes concealed these facts, which were so important, and pretending that the alliance was to be brought about, not through the crisis, but through his own negotiations, [142] first he persuaded the people to give up all consideration of the terms of the alliance, and to count themselves fortunate if only it were made;

Demosthenes' three mistakes

i. Compare Demosthenes *On the Crown* §178

and when he had gained this point he betrayed all Boeotia to the Thebans by writing in the decree, "If any city refuse to follow Thebes, the Athenians shall aid the Boeotians in Thebes," cheating with words and altering the facts, as he is wont to do; as though, forsooth, when the Boeotians should be suffering in fact, they would be content with Demosthenes' fine phrases, rather than indignant at the outrageous way in which they had been treated; [143] and, secondly, he laid two thirds of the costs of the war upon you, whose danger was more remote, and only one third on the Thebans (in all this acting for bribes); and the leadership by sea he caused to be shared equally by both; but all the expenditure he laid upon you; and the leadership by land, if we are not to talk nonsense, he carried away bodily and handed it over to Thebes. The result was that in all the war that followed, Stratocles, your general, had no authority to plan for the safety of his troops. [144] And it is not true that in this I alone accuse, while others are silent; nay, I speak, all men blame him, you know the facts—and are not angry! For this is your experience as regards Demosthenes: you have so long been accustomed to hear of his crimes that they no longer surprise you. But it ought not so to be; you ought to be indignant, and to punish him, if the city is to prosper in the future.

Compare Demosthenes' *On the Crown* §238

[145] But he was guilty of a second and far greater crime; for he stole the senate-house of the city and the democracy outright and carried them off to Thebes, to the Cadmeia, by his agreement with the Boeotarchs for joint control. And he contrived such domination for himself that now he came forward to the platform and declared that he was going as ambassador wherever he chose, whether you sent him or not; and, treating your magistrates as his slaves, and teaching them to raise no word of opposition against him, he declared that [146] if any of the generals should oppose him, he would bring

ii. Compare Demosthenes *On the Crown* §§178–79

suit to settle the claims of the speakers' platform as
against those of the war office; for he said you owed
more benefits to him from the platform than to the generals from the war office. And by drawing pay for empty
places in the mercenary force, by stealing the pay of
the troops, and by hiring out those ten thousand mercenaries to the Amphissians against my repeated protests
and complaints in the assembly—when the mercenaries
had thus been carried off, he rushed the city all unprepared into the midst of peril. [147] What, think you,
would Philip have prayed for at that crisis? Would it
not have been that he might in one place fight against
the city's forces, and in another, in Amphissa, against the
mercenaries, and thus close his hand upon the Greeks
already discouraged by so great a disaster? And Demosthenes, who is responsible for such misfortunes as that,
is not content with escaping punishment, but is miserable
unless he shall be crowned with a golden crown! Nor is
he satisfied that the crown shall be announced in your
presence, but if it is not to be proclaimed before the
Hellenes, he is miserable over that. So true it seems to
be that a wicked nature, when it has laid hold on great
license, works out public disaster.

[148] But the third and greatest of the crimes that I
have mentioned is that which I am about to describe.
Philip did not despise the Greeks, and he was well aware
(for he was not without understanding) that he was
about to contend in a little fraction of a day for all that
he possessed; for that reason he wished to make peace,
and was on the point of sending envoys. The officials at
Thebes also were frightened at the impending danger—
naturally, for they had no run-away orator and deserter
to advise them, but the ten years' Phocian war had
taught them a lesson not to be forgotten. [149] Now
when Demosthenes saw that such was the situation,
suspecting that the Boeotarchs were about to conclude

iii. Never
directly
refuted by
Demosthenes

356–46 B.C.

142

a separate peace and get gold from Philip without his being in it, and thinking that life was not worth living if he was to be left out of any act of bribery, he jumped up in the assembly, when no man was saying a word either in favour of making peace with Philip or against it; and with the idea of serving a sort of notice on the Boeotarchs that they must turn over to him his share of the gain, he swore by Athena [150] (whose statue, it seems, Pheidias wrought expressly that Demosthenes might have it to perjure himself by and to make profit of) that if any one should say that we ought to make peace with Philip, he would seize him by the hair and drag him to prison—in this imitating the politics of Cleophon, who, they tell us, in the time of the war against the Lacedaemonians, brought ruin to the state. But when the officials in Thebes would pay no attention to him, but even turned your soldiers back again when they had marched out, for they wished to give you an opportunity to deliberate concerning peace, [151] then indeed he became frantic, and went forward to the platform and stigmatized the Boeotarchs as traitors to Hellas, and declared that he would move a decree—he, who never looked on the face of an enemy in arms!—that you should send ambassadors to Thebes to ask them to give you free passage through their country for the march against Philip. But the officials in Thebes, ashamed lest they should seem in reality to be traitors to Hellas, turned from the thought of peace, and threw themselves into the war.

[152] Here indeed it is fitting that we should pay the tribute of memory to those brave men whom he, regardless of the smouldering and ill-omened sacrifices, sent forth into manifest danger—he who, when they had fallen, dared to set his cowardly and run-away feet upon their tomb and eulogise the valour of the dead. O man of all mankind most useless for great and serious deeds,

The threat of a separate peace

An Athenian demagogue who rejected the Spartan peace offer of 405 B.C.

Compare Demosthenes On the Crown §285

but for boldness of words most wonderful, will you presently undertake to look this jury in the face and say that over the disasters of the city you must be crowned? And, gentlemen, if he does, will you endure it? Are we to believe that you and your memory are to die with the dead? [153] I ask you to imagine for a little time that you are not in the court-room, but in the theatre, and to imagine that you see the herald coming forward to make the proclamation under the decree; consider whether you believe the relatives of the dead will shed more tears over the tragedies and the sufferings of the heroes soon afterward to be presented on the stage, or over the blindness of the city. [154] For what Greek, nurtured in freedom, would not mourn as he sat in the theatre and recalled this, if nothing more, that once on this day, when as now the tragedies were about to be performed, in a time when the city had better customs and followed better leaders, the herald would come forward and place before you the orphans whose fathers had died in battle, young men clad in the panoply of war; and he would utter that proclamation so honourable and so incentive to valour: "These young men, whose fathers showed themselves brave men and died in war, have been supported by the state until they have come of age; and now, clad thus in full armour by their fellow citizens, they are sent out with the prayers of the city, to go each his way; and they are invited to seats of honour in the theatre." [155] This was the proclamation then, but not to-day. For when the herald has led forward the man who is responsible for making the children orphans, what will he proclaim? What words will he utter? For if he shall recite the mere dictates of the decree, yet the truth, ashamed, will refuse to be silent, and we shall seem to hear it crying out in words which contradict the voice of the herald, "This man, if man he can be called, the Athenian people crown, the basest—

'for his virtue'; and 'for his nobility'—the coward and deserter." [156] No! by Zeus and the gods, do not, my fellow citizens, do not, I beseech you, set up in the orchestra of Dionysus a memorial of your own defeat; do not in the presence of the Greeks convict the Athenian people of having lost their reason; do not remind the poor Thebans of their incurable and irreparable disasters, men who, exiled through Demosthenes' acts, found refuge with you, when their shrines and children and tombs had been destroyed by Demosthenes' taking of bribes and by the Persian gold. [157] But since you were not present in person, yet in imagination behold their disaster; imagine that you see their city taken, the razing of their walls, the burning of their homes; their women and children led into captivity; their old men, their aged matrons, late in life learning to forget what freedom means; weeping, supplicating you, angry not so much at those who are taking vengeance upon them, as at the men who are responsible for it all; and calling on you by no means to crown the curse of Hellas, but rather to guard yourselves against the evil genius and the fate that ever pursue the man. [158] For there is no city, there is no private man—not one—that has ever come off safe after following Demosthenes' counsel. You have passed a law, fellow citizens, governing the men who steer the boats across the strait to Salamis; if one of them by accident overturns a boat in the strait, your law permits him no longer to be a ferryman, in order that no man may be careless of Greek lives; are you not then ashamed if this man, who has utterly overturned the city and all Hellas, if this man is to be permitted again to pilot the ship of state?

> Compare
> Demosthenes
> *On the Crown*
> §41

[159] But that I may speak concerning the fourth period also, and the present situation, I wish to remind you of this fact, that Demosthenes not only deserted his post in the army, but his post in the city also; for he

> Period Four:
> §§159–67

145

Compare
Demosthenes
On the Crown
§248

After Philip
spared Athens

took possession of one of your triremes and levied money upon the Greeks. But when our unexpected safety had brought him back to the city, during the first months the man was timid, and he came forward half-dead to the platform and urged you to elect him "preserver of the peace." But as for you, you would not even let resolutions that were passed bear the name of Demosthenes as the mover, but gave that honour to Nausicles. And yet, to-day, here is Demosthenes actually demanding a crown!

336 B.C.

Philip's
murderer

[160] But when Philip was dead and Alexander had come to the throne, Demosthenes again put on prodigious airs and caused a shrine to be dedicated to Pausanias and involved the senate in the charge of having offered sacrifice of thanksgiving as for good news. And he nicknamed Alexander "Margites"; and had the effrontery to say that Alexander would never stir out of Macedonia, for he was content, he said, to saunter around in Pella, and keep watch over the omens; and he said this statement was not based on conjecture, but on accurate knowledge, for valour was to be purchased at the price of blood. For Demosthenes, having no blood himself, formed his judgment of Alexander, not from Alexander's nature, but from his own cowardice. [161] But when now the Thessalians had voted to march against our city, and the young Alexander was at first bitterly angry—naturally—and when the army was near Thebes, Demosthenes, who had been elected ambassador by you, turned back when half-way across Cithaeron and came running home—useless in peace and war alike! And worst of all: while you did not surrender him nor allow him to be brought to trial in the synod of the Greeks, he has betrayed you now, if current report is true. [162] For, as the people of the Paralus say, and those who have been ambassadors to Alexander—and the story is sufficiently credible—there is one Aristion, a

The Athenians' official
dispatch ship

man of Plataean status, son of Aristobulus the apothecary, known perhaps to some of you. This young man, distinguished for extraordinary beauty of person, once lived a long time in Demosthenes' house (what he used to do there or what was done to him, is a scandal that is in dispute, and the story is one that would be quite improper for me to repeat). Now I am told that this Aristion, his origin and personal history being unknown to the king, is worming himself into favour with Alexander and getting access to him. Through him Demosthenes has sent a letter to Alexander, and has secured a certain degree of immunity for himself, and reconciliation; and he has carried his flattery to great lengths.

[163] But see from the following how the facts tally with the charge. For if Demosthenes had been bent on war with Alexander, as he claims to have been, or had any thought of it, three of the best opportunities in the world have been offered to him, and, as you see, he has not seized one of them. One, the first, was when Alexander, newly come to the throne, and not yet fairly settled in his personal affairs, crossed into Asia. The king of Persia was at the height of his power then, with ships and money and troops, and he would gladly have received us into his alliance because of the dangers that were threatening him. But did you, Demosthenes, at that time say a word? Did you move a decree? Shall I assume that you followed your natural disposition and were frightened? And yet the public opportunity waits not for the orator's fears. [164] But when Darius was come down to the coast with all his forces, and Alexander was shut up in Cilicia in extreme want, as you yourself said, and was, according to your statement, on the point of being trampled under the hoofs of the Persian horse, and when there was not room enough in the city to contain your odious demonstrations and the letters that you carried around, dangling them from your fingers,

Three lost
opportunities:

i. When
Persia would
have allied
with us vs.
Alexander

ii. When
Alexander
was in Cilicia
(333 B.C.)

while you pointed to my face as showing my discouragement and consternation, and in anticipation of some mishap to Alexander you called me "gilded-horn," and said the garland was already on my head, not even then did you take one step, but deferred it all for some more favourable opportunity.

I.e., sacrificial beast

A third opportunity, continues Aeschines, came not long ago (331 B.C.) when Sparta led a Peloponnesian revolt against Macedon. This too Demosthenes might have used to show his opposition to Alexander, if he was truly his enemy. But, in fact, he is neither anti-Macedonian, nor a friend of the people. His whole background is sordid:

iii. When Alexander was engaged against Sparta

[171] His father was Demosthenes of Paeania, a free man, for there is no need of lying. But how the case stands as to his inheritance from his mother and his maternal grandfather, I will tell you. There was a certain Gylon of Cerameis. This man betrayed Nymphaeum in the Pontus to the enemy, for the place at that time belonged to our city. He was impeached and became an exile from the city, not awaiting trial. He came to Bosporus and there received as a present from the tyrants of the land a place called "the Gardens." [172] Here he married a woman who was rich, I grant you, and brought him a big dowry, but a Scythian by blood. This wife bore him two daughters, whom he sent hither with plenty of money. One he married to a man whom I will not name—for I do not care to incur the enmity of many persons,—the other, in contempt of the laws of the city, Demosthenes of Paeania took to wife. She it was who bore your busy-body and informer. From his grandfather, therefore, he would inherit enmity toward the people, for you condemned his ancestors to death; and by his mother's blood he would be a Scythian, a Greek-tongued barbarian—so that his knavery, too, is no product of our soil. [173] But in daily life what is

Demosthenes' mother; compare the insults in On the Crown *§§259 and 260*

he? From being a trierarch he suddenly came forward as a hired writer of speeches, when he had disreputably squandered his patrimony. But when he had lost his reputation even in this profession, for he disclosed his client's arguments to their opponents, he vaulted on to the political platform. And though he made enormous profits out of politics, he laid up next to nothing. It is true that just now the Persian's gold has floated his extravagance, but even that will not suffice, for no wealth ever yet kept up with a debauched character. And to sum it all up, he supplies his wants, not from his private income, but from your perils.

> The last quarter of the speech is a series of loosely connected topics—admonitions against excessive awards of honor, attacks on the present reluctance to convict accused criminals, warnings and refutations in anticipation of the defence, invective against Ctesiphon and Demosthenes. Finally he concludes with a widely admired peroration and a less highly esteemed concluding paragraph:

[257] But when at last at the close of his speech he calls forward to support his cause the men who have shared his bribes, imagine that on the platform where now I am standing as I speak, you see, drawn up in array against the lawlessness of these men, the benefactors of the state: Solon, who equipped the democracy with the best of laws, a philosopher and a good lawgiver, begging you soberly, as he naturally would, by no means to hold the words of Demosthenes as more weighty than your oaths and the laws; and that man who assessed the tribute of the Greeks, and whose daughters our people dowered after his death, [258] Aristides, expressing his indignation at this mockery of justice, and asking you if you are not ashamed that

Peroration

"So fine a peroration is perhaps not in any language to be found."—Lord Brougham

149

whereas, when Arthmius of Zeleia transported the gold of the Medes into Hellas, although he had once resided in our city, and was proxenus of the Athenian people, your fathers were all but ready to kill him, and they warned him out of their city, and out of all the territory under Athenian control, [259] you now propose to crown with a golden crown Demosthenes, a man who has not indeed "transported" the gold of the Medes, but has received it as a bribe, and keeps it to this day. Think you not that Themistocles and those who died at Marathon and at Plataea, and the very sepulchres of your fathers, will groan aloud, if the man who admits that he has negotiated with the barbarians against the Greeks shall receive a crown?

[260] Be ye my witnesses, O Earth and Sun, and Virtue and Conscience, and Education, by which we distinguish the honourable and the base, that I have heard my country's call, and have spoken. If I have presented the accusations well and in a manner commensurate with the crime, I have spoken according to my desire; if insufficiently, according to my ability. It remains for you, fellow citizens, in view both of what has been spoken and what is left unsaid, yourselves to give the verdict that is just and for the city's good.

Coda

". . . a total failure. . . ."
—Lord Brougham

From the
ADDRESS ON THE CROWN
OF DEMOSTHENES

INTRODUCTION

Aeschines must have felt he had some grounds for confidence in 330 B.C. when he renewed his attack on Demosthenes by the indirect method of prosecuting Ctesiphon. Demosthenes' policies had obviously failed, his predictions about the conduct of Macedon were clearly wrong, and while Demosthenes' influence at home seemed to have dwindled, abroad Philip's son and successor, Alexander, in his expedition against the Persian empire was proving himself the most successful general Greece had ever seen. But in striking at Demosthenes Aeschines failed to weigh properly two important factors: the extent and the bitterness of the Athenian feeling against Macedon, and the power of Demosthenes' oratory.

The reply that Demosthenes made to Aeschines' charges has often been considered his masterpiece. Surely few passages in any literature can rival the vividness of his narrative of the moment when the news of Philip's seizure of Elateia reached Athens (§§169 ff.) or the fervor of his appeal to the heritage of Athens (§§ 202 ff.). After hearing this speech the jury not only voted to acquit Ctesiphon but so completely repudiated the prosecution that Aeschines was fined under that provision of Athenian law which penalized a prosecutor if he failed to win one fifth of the votes. For Aeschines his attack on Demosthenes had amounted to political suicide. After the trial he left Athens and never returned: Demosthenes remained in Athens persisting in the opposition to Macedon that was to cost him his life in 322 B.C.

The manuscripts of Demosthenes often provide texts which purport to be the documents, decrees, lists, and so forth that Demosthenes asked to be read to the jury. Since some of these records are demonstrably the falsifications of an age long after Demosthenes, and since none is unquestionably authentic, Pickard-Cambridge, the translator of this speech, has omitted them from his text.

After a proem in which he appeals for a favorable hearing and promises to deal with all Aeschines' charges, Demosthenes commences what is in effect a long discursive narrative of the events from the time of the war with Philip in the 350's down to the aftermath of Athens' defeat at Chaeronea in 338 B.C. The first part of this account is a justification of Demosthenes' role in the events immediately preceding and folowing the peace with Macedon in 346 B.C. He says he is especially anxious to examine the false statements which Aeschines

On the Peace
of Philocrates
346 B.C.

[17] made against me in regard to the Peace and the Embassy, when he ascribed to me the things which he himself had done in conjunction with Philocrates. And here it is necessary, men of Athens, and perhaps appropriate, that I should remind you of the state of affairs subsisting during that period, so that you may view each group of actions in the light of the circumstances of the time.

356 B.C.

[18] When the Phocian war had broken out (not through any action of mine, for I had not yet entered public life), your own attitude, in the first place, was such, that you wished for the preservation of the Phocians, although you saw that their actions were unjustifiable; while you would have been delighted at anything that might happen to the Thebans, against whom you felt an indignation that was neither unrea-

sonable nor unfair; for they had not used their good
fortune at Leuctra with moderation. And, in the second
place, the Peloponnese was all disunited: those who
detested the Spartans were not strong enough to annihilate them, and those who had previously governed with
the support of Sparta were no longer able to maintain
their control over their cities; but both these and all the
other states were in a condition of indeterminate strife
and confusion. [19] When Philip saw this (for it was
not hard to see), he tried, by dispensing money to the
traitors whom each state contained, to throw them all
into collision and stir up one against another; and thus,
amid the blunders and perversity of others, he was
making his own preparations, and growing great to the
danger of all. And when it became clear to all that the
then overbearing (but now unhappy) Thebans, dis-
tressed by the length of the war, would be forced to
fly to you for aid, Philip, to prevent this—to prevent the
formation of any union between the cities—made offers
of peace to you, and of assistance to them. [20] Now
what was it that helped him, and enabled him to find in
you his almost willing dupes? It was the baseness (if
that is the right name to use), or the ignorance, or both,
of the rest of the Hellenes, who, though you were engaged in a long and continuous war, and that on behalf
of the interests of all, as has been proved by the event,
never assisted you either with money or with men, or
in any other way whatsoever. And in your just and
proper indignation with them, you listened readily to
Philip. It was for these reasons, therefore, and not
through any action of mine, that the Peace which we
then conceded was negotiated; and any one who in-
vestigates the matter honestly will find that it is the
crimes and the corrupt practices of these men, in the
course of the negotiations, that are responsible for our
position to-day. [21] It is in the interests of truth that I

enter into all these events with this exactitude and thoroughness; for however strong the appearance of criminality in these proceedings may be, it has, I imagine, nothing to do with me. The first man to suggest or mention the Peace was Aristodemus the actor; and the person who took the matter up and moved the motion, and sold his services for the purpose, along with Aeschines, was Philocrates of Hagnus—your partner, Aeschines, not mine, even if you split your sides with lying; while those who supported him, from whatever motive (for of that I say nothing at present), were Eubulus and Cephisophon. I had no part in the matter anywhere. [22] And yet, although the facts are such as with absolute truth I am representing them to be, he carried his effrontery so far as to dare to assert that I was not only responsible for the Peace, but had also prevented the city from acting in conjunction with a general assembly of the Hellenes in making it. What? and you —oh! how can one find a name that can be applied to you?—when you saw me (for you were there) preventing the city from taking this great step and forming so grand an alliance as you just now described, did you once raise a protest or come forward to give information and to set forth the crimes with which you now charge me? [23] If I had covenanted with Philip for money that I would prevent the coalition of the Hellenes, your only course was to refuse to keep silence—to cry aloud, to protest, to reveal the fact to your fellow countrymen. On no occasion did you do this: no such utterance of yours was ever heard by any one. In fact there was no embassy away at the time on a mission to any Hellenic state; the Hellenes had all long ago been tried and found wanting; and in all that he has said upon this matter there is not a single sound word. [24] And, apart from that, his falsehoods involve the greatest calumnies upon this city. For if you were at one and the same time convoking the

The events of
347–46 B.C.

Compare
Aeschines
*Against
Ctesiphon* §62

Compare
Aeschines
§63

Compare
Aeschines
§58

Hellenes with a view to war, and sending ambassadors yourselves to Philip to discuss peace, it was a deed for a Eurybatus, not a task for a state or for honest men, that you were carrying out. But that is not the case; indeed it is not. For what could possibly have been your object in summoning them at that moment? Was it with a view to peace? But they all had peace already. Or with a view to war? But you were yourselves discussing peace. It is therefore evident that neither was it I that introduced or was responsible for the Peace in its original shape, nor is one of all the other falsehoods which he told of me shown to be true.

[25] Again, consider the course of action which, when the city had concluded the Peace, each of us now chose to adopt. For from this you will know who it was that co-operated with Philip throughout, and who it was that acted in your interest and sought the good of the city. As for me, I proposed, as a member of the Council, that the ambassadors should sail as quickly as possible to any district in which they should ascertain Philip to be, and receive his oath from him. But even when I had carried this resolution, they would not act upon it. [26] What did this mean, men of Athens? I will inform you. Philip's interest required that the interval before he took the oath should be as long as possible; yours, that it should be as short as possible. And why? Because you broke off all your preparations for the war, not merely from the day when he took the oath, but from the day when you first hoped that Peace would be made; and for his part, this was what he was all along working for; for he thought (and with truth) that whatever places he could snatch from Athens before he took the oath, would remain securely his, since no one would break the Peace for their sake. [27] Foreseeing and calculating upon this, men of Athens, I proposed this decree—that we should sail to any district in which Philip might be,

The parties to the peace were to retain the territory they held at the time of swearing

155

and receive his oath as soon as possible, in order that the oaths might be taken while the Thracians, your allies, were still in possession of those strongholds of which Aeschines just now spoke with contempt—Serrhium, Myrtenum, and Ergiske; and that Philip might not snatch from us the keys of the country and make himself master of Thrace, nor obtain an abundant supply of money and of soldiers, and so proceed without difficulty to the prosecution of his further designs. [28] And now, instead of citing or reading this decree he slanders me on the ground that I thought fit, as a member of the Council, to introduce the envoys. But what should I have done? Was I to propose *not* to introduce those who had come for the express purpose of speaking with you? or to order the lessee of the theatre not to assign them seats? But they would have watched the play from the threepenny seats if this decree had not been proposed. Should I have guarded the interests of the city in petty details, and sold them wholesale, as my opponents did? Surely not. (*To the clerk.*) Now take this decree, which the prosecutor passed over, though he knew it well, and read it.

Compare
Aeschines
§68

[29]   [*The decree of Demosthenes is read.*]

[30] Though I had carried this decree, and was seeking the good not of Philip, but of the city, these worthy ambassadors paid little heed to it, but sat idle in Macedonia for three whole months, until Philip arrived from Thrace, after subduing the whole country; when they might, within ten days, or equally well within three or four, have reached the Hellespont, and saved the strongholds, by receiving his oath before he could seize them. For he would not have touched them when we were present; or else, if he had done so, we should have refused to administer the oath to him; and in that case

Negligence
of the
ambassadors

he would have failed to obtain the Peace: he would not have had both the Peace and the strongholds as well.

[31] Such was Philip's first act of fraud, during the time of the Embassy, and the first instance of venality on the part of these wicked men; and over this I confess that then and now and always I have been and am at war and at variance with them. Now observe, immediately after this, a second and even greater piece of villainy. [32] As soon as Philip had sworn to the Peace, after first gaining possession of Thrace because these men did not obey my decree, he obtained from them—again by purchase—the postponement of our departure from Macedonia, until all should be in readiness for his campaign against the Phocians; in order that, instead of our bringing home a report of his intentions and his preparations for the march, which would make you set out and sail round to Thermopylae with your war-ships as you did before, you might only hear our report of the facts when he was already on this side of Thermopylae, and you could do nothing. [33] And Philip was beset with such fear and such a weight of anxiety, lest in spite of his occupation of these places, his object should slip from his grasp, if, before the Phocians were destroyed, you resolved to assist them, that he hired this despicable creature, not now in company with his colleagues, but by himself alone, to make to you a statement and a report of such a character that owing to them all was lost. [34] But I request and entreat you, men of Athens, to remember throughout this whole trial, that, had Aeschines made no accusation that was not included in the indictment, I too would not have said a word that did not bear upon it; but since he has had recourse to all kinds of imputation and slander at once, I am compelled also to give a brief answer to each group of charges. [35] What then were the statements uttered by him that day, in consequence of which all

Aeschines'
second
treachery

was lost? 'You must not be perturbed,' he said, 'at Philip's having crossed to this side of Thermopylae; for you will get everything that you desire, if you remain quiet; and within two or three days you will hear that he has become the friend of those whose enemy he was, and the enemy of those whose friend he was, when he first came. For,' said he, 'it is not phrases that confirm friendships' (a finely sententious expression!) 'but identity of interest; and it is to the interest of Philip and of the Phocians and of yourselves alike, to be rid of the heartless and overbearing demeanour of the Thebans.'

Feeling against Thebes in 346 B.C.

[36] To these statements some gave a ready ear, in consequence of the tacit ill-feeling towards the Thebans at the time. What then followed—and not after a long interval, but immediately? The Phocians were overthrown; their cities were razed to the ground; you, who had believed Aeschines and remained inactive, were soon afterwards bringing in your effects from the country; while Aeschines received his gold; and besides all this, the city reaped the ill-will of the Thebans and Thessalians, while their gratitude for what had been done went to Philip. [37] To prove that this is so (*to the clerk*) read me both the decree of Callisthenes, and Philip's letter. (*To the jury.*) These two documents together will make all the facts plain. (*To the clerk.*) Read.

[38]   [*The decree of Callisthenes is read.*]

Were these the hopes, on the strength of which you made the Peace? Was this what this hireling promised you? [39] (*To the clerk.*) Now read the letter which Philip sent after this.

[*Philip's letter is read.*]

[40] You hear how obviously, in this letter sent to you, Philip is addressing definite information to his own allies. 'I have done these things,' he tells them, 'against

158

the will of the Athenians, and to their annoyance; and so, men of Thebes and Thessaly, if you are wise, you will regard them as enemies, and will trust me.' He does not write in those actual terms, but that is what he intends to indicate. By these means he so carried them away, that they did not foresee or realize any of the consequences, but allowed him to get everything into his own power: and that is why, poor men, they have experienced their present calamities. [41] But the man who helped him to create this confidence, who co-operated with him, who brought home that false report and deluded you, he it is who now bewails the sufferings of the Thebans and enlarges upon their piteousness—he, who is himself the cause both of these and of the misery in Phocis, and of all the other evils which the Hellenes have endured. Yes, it is evident that you are pained at what has come to pass, Aeschines, and that you are sorry for the Thebans, when you have property in Boeotia and are farming the land that was theirs; and that I rejoice at it—I, whose surrender was immediately demanded by the author of the disaster! [42] But I have digressed into subjects of which it will perhaps be more convenient to speak presently. I will return to the proofs which show that it is the crimes of these men that are the cause of our condition to-day.

The feeling for Thebes now

For when you had been deceived by Philip, through the agency of these men, who while serving as ambassadors had sold themselves and made a report in which there was not a word of truth—when the unhappy Phocians had been deceived and their cities annihilated—what followed? [43] The despicable Thessalians and the slow-witted Thebans regarded Philip as their friend, their benefactor, their saviour. Philip was their all-in-all. They would not even listen to the voice of any one who wished to express a different opinion. You yourselves, though you viewed what had been done with suspicion and vexation, nevertheless kept the Peace; for there was nothing else that you could have done. And the other Hellenes, who, like yourselves, had been deluded and disappointed of their hopes, also kept the Peace, and gladly; since in a sense they also were remotely aimed at by the war.

> Demosthenes soon turns to attacking Aeschines as a traitor hired by Philip for the subversion of Athens. He then has Aeschines' indictment of Ctesiphon read and proceeds to deal with its clauses. Aeschines' assertion that the praise of Demosthenes as one who "keeps doing what is good for the people" is false leads Demosthenes into a discussion of the policy that he advocated for dealing with Philip:

354 B.C.

[60] I will pass over all that Philip snatched from us and secured, in the days before I took part in public life as an orator. None of these losses, I imagine, has anything to do with me. But I will recall to you, and will render you an account of all that, from the day when I entered upon this career, he was *prevented* from taking, when I have made one remark. [61] Philip, men of Athens, had a great advantage in his favour. For in the midst of the Hellenic peoples—and not of some only, but of all alike—there had sprung up a crop of traitors—corrupt, god-forsaken men—more numerous than they have ever been within the memory of man. These he took to help and co-operate with him; and great as the mutual ill-will and dissensions of the Hellenes already were, he rendered them even worse, by deceiving some, making presents to others, and corrupting others in every way; and at a time when all had in reality but one interest—to prevent his becoming powerful—he divided them into a number of factions. [62] All the Hellenes then being in this condition, still ignorant of the growing and accumulating evil, you have to ask your-

selves, men of Athens, what policy and action it was fitting for the city to choose, and to hold me responsible for this; for the person who assumed that responsibility in the State was myself. [63] Should she, Aeschines, have sacrificed her pride and her own dignity? Should she have joined the ranks of the Thessalians and Dolopes, and helped Philip to acquire the empire of Hellas, cancelling thereby the noble and righteous deeds of our forefathers? Or, if she should not have done this (for it would have been in very truth an atrocious thing), should she have looked on, while all that she saw would happen, if no one prevented it—all that she realized, it seems, at a distance—was actually taking place? [64] Nay, I should be glad to ask to-day the severest critic of my actions, which party he would have desired the city to join—the party which shares the responsibility for the misery and disgrace which has fallen upon the Hellenes (the party of the Thessalians and their supporters, one may call it), or the party which looked on while these calamities were taking place, in the hope of gaining some advantage for themselves—in which we should place the Arcadians and Messenians and Argives. [65] But even of these, many—nay, all—have in the end fared worse than we. For if Philip had departed immediately after his victory, and gone his way; if afterwards he had remained at peace, and had given no trouble whatever to any of his own allies or of the other Hellenes; then there would have been some ground for blaming and accusing those who had opposed his plans. But if he has stripped them all alike of their dignity, their paramountcy, and their independence— nay, even of their free constitutions, wherever he could do so—can it be denied that the policy which you adopted on my advice was the most glorious policy possible?

[66] But I return to my former point. What was it

Philip's satellites

The "unaligned"

Battle of Chaeronea, 338 B.C.

fitting for the city to do, Aeschines, when she saw Philip establishing for himself a despotic sway over the Hellenes? What language should have been used, what measures proposed, by the adviser of the people at Athens (for that it was at Athens makes the utmost difference), when I knew that from the very first, up to the day when I myself ascended the platform, my country had always contended for pre-eminence, honour, and glory, and in the cause of honour, and for the interests of all, had sacrificed more money and lives than any other Hellenic people had spent for their private ends: [67] when I saw that Philip himself, with whom our conflict lay, for the sake of empire and absolute power, had had his eye knocked out, his collarbone broken, his hand and his leg maimed, and was ready to resign any part of his body that Fortune chose to take from him, provided that with what remained he might live in honour and glory? [68] And surely no one would dare to say that it was fitting that in one bred at Pella, a place then inglorious and insignificant, there should have grown up so lofty a spirit that he aspired after the empire of Hellas, and conceived such a project in his mind; but that in you, who are Athenians, and who day by day in all that you hear and see behold the memorials of the gallantry of your forefathers, such baseness should be found, that you would yield up your liberty to Philip by your own deliberate offer and deed. [69] No man would say this. One alternative remained, and that, one which you were bound to take—that of a righteous resistance to the whole course of action by which he was doing you injury. You acted thus from the first, quite rightly and properly; while I helped by my proposals and advice during the time of my political activity, and I do not deny it. But what ought I to have done? For the time has come to ask you this, Aeschines, and to dismiss everything else. [70] Amphipolis, Pydna,

Potidaea, Halonnesus—all are blotted from my memory.
As for Serrhium, Doriscus, the sack of Peparethus, and
all the other injuries inflicted upon the city, I renounce
all knowledge of their ever having happened—though
you actually said that *I* involved my countrymen in
hostility by talking of these things, when the decrees
which deal with them were the work of Eubulus and
Aristophon and Diopeithes, and not mine at all—so
glibly do you assert anything that suits your purpose!
[71] But of this too I say nothing at present. I only ask
you whether Philip, who was appropriating Euboea,
and establishing it as a stronghold to command Attica;
who was making an attempt upon Megara, seizing Oreus, razing the walls of Porthmus, setting up Philistides
as tyrant at Oreus and Cleitarchus at Eretria, bringing
the Hellespont into his own power, besieging Byzantium,
destroying some of the cities of Hellas, and restoring his
exiled friends to others—whether he, I say, in acting
thus, was guilty of wrong, violating the truce and breaking the Peace, or not? Was it fit that one of the Hellenes should arise to prevent it, or not? [72] If it was
not fit—if it was fit that Hellas should become like the
Mysian booty in the proverb before men's eyes, while the
Athenians had life and being, then I have lost my labour in speaking upon this theme, and the city has lost
its labour in obeying me: then let everything that has
been done be counted for a crime and a blunder, and
those my own! But if it was right that one should arise
to prevent it, for whom could the task be more fitting
than for the people of Athens? That then, was the aim
of *my* policy; and when I saw Philip reducing all mankind to servitude, I opposed him, and without ceasing
warned and exhorted you to make no surrender.

> Aeschines' charge that Demosthenes brought on
> the last disastrous war with Philip is too damaging
> to let pass without a detailed refutation. De-

Compare
Aeschines §82

Philip's
activities,
346–40 B.C.

mosthenes cites documents in an effort to support
his contention that the war was not his responsibility. He refers to a letter of Philip in order
to show that even *he* did not blame Demosthenes
for the war. Then he explains exactly what he
did do in the period from the Peace of Philocrates to the outbreak of the new war with
Philip:

[79] First of all, when he was trying to steal into
the Peloponnese, I proposed the embassy to the Peloponnese; then, when he was grasping at Euboea, the
embassy to Euboea; then the expedition—not an embassy any more—to Oreus, and that to Eretria, when he
had established tyrants in those cities. [80] After that

341 B.C.

I dispatched all the naval expeditions, in the course of
which the Chersonese and Byzantium and all our allies
were saved. In consequence of this, the noblest rewards
at the hands of those who had benefited by your action
became yours—votes of thanks, glory, honours, crowns,
gratitude; while of the victims of his aggression, those
who followed your advice at the time secured their own
deliverance, and those who neglected it had the memory
of your warnings constantly in their minds, and regarded you not merely as their well-wishers, but as men
of wisdom and prophetic insight; for all that you fore-
told has come to pass. [81] And further, that Philistides
would have given a large sum to retain Oreus, and
Cleitarchus to retain Eretria, and Philip himself, to be
able to count upon the use of these places against you,
and to escape all exposure of his other proceedings and
all investigation, by any one in any place, of his wrongful acts—all this is not unknown to any one, least of all
to you, Aeschines. [82] For the envoys sent at that time
by Cleitarchus and Philistides lodged at your house,
when they came here, and you acted as their patron.
Though the city rejected them, as enemies whose pro-

posals were neither just nor expedient, to you they were friends. None of their attempts succeeded, slander me though you may, when you assert that I say nothing when I receive money, but cry out when I spend it. That, certainly, is not *your* way: for you cry out with money in your hands, and will never cease, unless those present cause you to do so by taking away your civil rights to-day. [83] Now on that occasion, gentlemen, you crowned me for my conduct. Aristonicus proposed a decree whose very syllables were identical with those of Ctesiphon's present proposal; the crown was proclaimed in the theatre; and this was already the second proclamation in my honour: and yet Aeschines, though he was there, neither opposed the decree, nor indicted the mover. (*To the clerk.*) Take this decree also and read it.

Demosthenes' earlier crowning, 340 B.C.

[84]   [*The decree of Aristonicus is read.*]

[85] Now is any of you aware of any discredit that attached itself to the city owing to this decree? Did any mockery or ridicule ensue, such as Aeschines said must follow on the present occasion, if I were crowned? But surely when proceedings are recent and well known to all, then it is that, if they are satisfactory, they meet with gratitude, and if they are otherwise, with punishment. It appears, then, that on that occasion I met with gratitude, not with blame or punishment.

[86] Thus the fact that, up to the time when these events took place, I acted throughout as was best for the city, has been acknowledged by the victory of my advice and my proposals in your deliberations, by the successful execution of the measures which I proposed, and the award of crowns in consequence of them to the city and to myself and to all, and by your celebration of sacrifices to the gods, and processions, in thankfulness for these blessings.

[87] When Philip had been expelled from Euboea—and while the arms which expelled him were yours, the statesmanship and the decrees (even though some of my opponents may split their sides) were mine—he proceeded to look for some other stronghold from which he could threaten the city. And seeing that we were more dependent than any other people upon imported corn, and wishing to get our corn-trade into his power, he advanced to Thrace. First, he requested the Byzantines, his own allies, to join him in the war against you; and when they refused and said (with truth) that they had not made their alliance with him for such a purpose, he erected a stockade against the city, brought up his engines, and proceeded to besiege it. [88] I will not ask again what you ought to have done when this was happening; it is manifest to all. But who was it that went to the rescue of the Byzantines, and saved them? Who was it that prevented the Hellespont from falling into other hands at that time? It was you, men of Athens—and when I say 'you,' I mean this city. And who was it that spoke and moved resolutions and acted for the city, and gave himself up unsparingly to the business of the State? It was I. [89] But of the immense benefit thus conferred upon all, you no longer need words of mine to tell you, since you have had actual experience of it. For the war which then ensued, apart from the glorious reputation that it brought you, kept you supplied with the necessaries of life in greater plenty and at lower prices than the present Peace, which these worthy men are guarding to their country's detriment, in their hopes of something yet to be realized.

Siege of
Byzantium,
340 B.C.

> Demosthenes turns from the alleged economic
> benefits of the policy of opposition to Philip to
> three other advantages:
> (1) The Chersonese and Byzantium were kept
>   out of Philip's hands.

(2) The city was honored with gold crowns by the grateful Byzantines and Chersonites.

(3) The nobility of Athens and the depravity of Philip were exposed to the whole world.

He then resumes his counter attack on Aeschines by discussing that politician's efforts to stir up old animosities between Athens and Euboea and Byzantium:

[95] In order to prove to you, also, that the slanders which he uttered against the Euboeans and Byzantines, as he recalled to you any ill-natured action that they had taken towards you in the past, are disingenuous calumnies, not only because they are false (for this, I think, you may all be assumed to know), but also because, however true they might be, it was still to your advantage to deal with the political situation as I have done, I desire to describe, and that briefly, one or two of the noble deeds which this city has done in your own time. For an individual and a State should strive always, in their respective spheres, to fashion their future conduct after the highest examples that their past affords. [96] Thus, men of Athens, at a time when the Spartans were masters of land and sea, and were retaining their hold, by means of governors and garrisons, upon the country all round Attica—Euboea, Tanagra, all Boeotia, Megara, Aegina, Ceos, and the other islands—and when Athens possessed neither ships nor walls, you marched forth to Haliartus, and again, not many days later, to Corinth, though the Athenians of that day might have borne a heavy grudge against both the Corinthians and the Thebans for the part they had played in reference to the Deceleian War. [97] But they bore no such grudge. Far from it! And neither of these actions, Aeschines, was taken by them to help benefactors; nor was the prospect before them free from danger. Yet they did not on that account sacrifice those who fled

The Corinthian War, 395–86 B.C.

Last part of the Peloponnesian War, 413–404 B.C.

to them for help. For the sake of glory and honour they were willing to expose themselves to the danger; and it was a right and a noble spirit that inspired their counsels. For the life of all men must end in death, though a man shut himself in a chamber and keep watch; but brave men must ever set themselves to do that which is noble, with their joyful hope for their buckler, and whatsoever God gives, must bear it gallantly. [98] Thus did your forefathers, and thus did the elder among yourselves: for, although the Spartans were no friends or benefactors of yours, but had done much grievous wrong to the city, yet, when the Thebans, after their victory at Leuctra, attempted to annihilate them, you prevented it, not terrified by the strength or the reputation which the Thebans then enjoyed, nor reckoning up what the men had done to you, for whom you were to face this peril. [99] And thus, as you know, you revealed to all the Hellenes, that whatever offences may be committed against you, though under all other circumstances you show your resentment of them, yet if any danger to life or freedom overtakes the transgressors, you will bear no grudge and make no reckoning. Nor was it in these instances only that you were thus disposed. For once more, when the Thebans were appropriating Euboea, you did not look on while it was done; you did not call to mind the wrong which had been done to you in the matter of Oropus by Themison and Theodorus: you helped even these; and it was then that the city for the first time had voluntary trierarchs, of whom I was one. But I will not speak of this yet. [100] And although to save the island was itself a noble thing to do, it was a yet nobler thing by far, that when their lives and their cities were absolutely in your power, you gave them back, as it was right to do, to the very men who had offended against you, and made no reckoning, when such trust had been placed in you,

Euboeans
who gave
Oropus to
Thebes

of the wrongs which you had suffered. I pass by the innumerable instances which I might still give—battles at sea, expeditions both long ago and now in our day; in all of which the object of the city has been to defend the freedom and safety of the other Hellenic peoples. [101] And so, when in all these striking examples I had beheld the city ever ready to strive in defence of the interests of others, what was I likely to bid her do, what action was I likely to recommend to her, when the debate to some extent concerned her own interests? 'Why,' you would say, 'to remember her grudge against those who wanted deliverance, and to look for excuses for sacrificing everything!' And who would not have been justified in putting me to death, if I had attempted to bring shame upon the city's high traditions, though it were only by word? The deed itself you would never have done, I know full well; for had you desired to do it, what was there to hinder you? Were you not free so to act? Had you not these men here to propose it?

[102] I wish now to return to the next in succession of my political acts; and here again you must ask yourselves, what was the best thing for the city? For, men of Athens, when I saw that your navy was breaking up, and that, while the rich were obtaining exemption on the strength of small payments, citizens of moderate or small means were losing all that they had; and further, that in consequence of these things the city was always missing her opportunities; I enacted a law in accordance with which I compelled the former—the rich—to do their duty fairly; I put an end to the injustice done to the poor, and (what was the greatest service of all to the State) I caused our preparations to be made in time. [103] When I was indicted for this, I appeared before you at the ensuing trial, and was acquitted; the prosecutor failed to obtain the necessary fraction of the votes. But what sums do you think the leaders of the Taxation-

Demosthenes'
naval reform,
340 B.C.

Boards, or those who stood second or third, offered me, to induce me, if possible, not to enact the law, or at least to let it drop and lie under sworn notice of prosecution? They offered sums so large, men of Athens, that I should hesitate to mention them to you. It was a natural course for them to take. [104] For under the former laws it was possible for them to divide their obligation between sixteen persons, paying little or nothing themselves, and grinding down their poorer fellow citizens: while by my law each must pay down a sum calculated in proportion to his property; and a man came to be charged with two warships, who had previously been one of sixteen subscribers to a single one (for they used now to call themselves no longer captains of their ships, but subscribers). Thus there was nothing that they were not willing to give, if only the new plan could be brought to nothing, and they could escape being compelled to do their duty fairly. (*To the clerk.*) [105] Now read me, first, the decree in accordance with which I had to meet the indictment; and then the lists of those liable under the former law, and under my own, respectively. Read.

[*The decree is read.*]

[106] Now produce that noble list.

[*A list is read.*]

Now produce, for comparison with this, the list under my own law.

[*A list is read.*]

"Poor"= least wealthy among the twelve hundred richest citizens

Was this, think you, but a trifling assistance which I rendered to the poor among you? [107] Would the wealthy have spent but a trifling sum to avoid doing their duty fairly? I am proud not only of having refused all compromise upon the measure, not only of having been acquitted when I was indicted, but also of having enacted a law which was beneficial, and of having given proof of it in practice. For throughout the war the armaments were equipped under my law, and no trierarch ever laid the suppliants' branch before you in token of grievance, nor took sanctuary at Munychia; none was imprisoned by the Admiralty Board; no warship was abandoned at sea and lost to the State, or left behind here as unseaworthy. Under the former laws all these things used to happen; [108] and the reason was that the obligation rested upon the poor, and in consequence there were many cases of inability to discharge it. I transferred the duties of the trierarchy from the poor to the rich; and therefore every duty was properly fulfilled. Aye, and for this very reason I deserve to receive praise—that I always adopted such political measures as brought with them accessions of glory and honour and power to the city. No measure of mine is malicious, harsh, or unprincipled; none is degrading or unworthy of the city. The same spirit will be seen both in my domestic and my international policy. [109] For just as in home affairs I did not set the favour of the rich above the rights of the many, so in international affairs I did not embrace the gifts and the friendship of Philip, in preference to the common interests of all the Hellenes.

[110] It still remains for me, I suppose, to speak about the proclamation, and about my examination. The statement that I acted for the best, and that I am loyal to you throughout and eager to do you good service, I have proved, I think, sufficiently, by what I have said. At the same time I am passing over the most important parts of my political life and actions; for I conceive that I ought first to render to you in their proper order my arguments in regard to the alleged illegality itself: which done, even if I say nothing about

The legality
of the
proclamation
of the crown

the rest of my political acts, I can still rely upon that personal knowledge of them which each of you possess.

Two of the technical points in Aeschines' indictment are now dealt with. First, Demosthenes argues, though rather cursorily, that it was proper for him to receive a vote of thanks for the donations he had made before he had undergone the examination and audit at the end of his term of office. Second, he contends, with stronger legal basis, that the decree of thanks could be proclaimed in the theatre. Then, once again, he lashes out at Aeschines:

Counterattack on Aeschines

[129] But although I am not at a loss to know what to say about you and yours, I am at a loss to know what to mention first. Shall I tell first how your father Tromes was a slave in the house of Elpias, who kept an elementary school near the temple of Theseus, and how he wore shackles and a wooden halter? Or how your mother, by celebrating her daylight nuptials in her hut near the shrine of the Hero of the Lancet was enabled to rear you, her beautiful statue, the prince of third-rate actors? But these things are known to all without my telling them. Shall I tell how Phormio, the ship's piper, the slave of Dion of Phrearrii, raised her up out of this noble profession? But, before God and every Heavenly Power, I shudder lest in using expressions which are fitly applied to you, I may be thought to have chosen a subject upon which it ill befits myself to speak. [130] So I will pass this by and will begin with the acts of his own life; for they were not like any chance actions, but such as the people curses. For only lately—lately, do I say? only yesterday or the day before—did he become at once an Athenian and an orator, and by the addition of two syllables converted his father from Tromes into Atrometus, and gave his mother the imposing name of Glaucothea, when every one knows

Thirteen years earlier Demosthenes called Aeschines "the son of Atrometus the teacher and Glaucothea"!

that she used to be called Empusa—a name which was | Hobgoblin
obviously given her because there was nothing that she
would not do or have done to her; for how else should
she have acquired it? [131] Yet, in spite of this, you are
of so ungrateful and villainous a nature, that though,
thanks to your countrymen, you have risen from slavery
to freedom, and from poverty to wealth, far from feeling gratitude to them, you devote your political activity
to working against them as a hireling. I will pass over
every case in which there is any room for the contention
that he has spoken in the interests of the city, and will
remind you of the acts which he was manifestly proved
to have done for the good of her enemies.

> Demosthenes alleges that Aeschines was impli-
> cated in several celebrated treasonous intrigues and
> then turns to discuss his role in the Amphictyonic
> deliberations of 339 B.C.:

[142] Why have I uttered this imprecation with
such vehemence and earnestness? Because, although I
have documents, lying in the public archives, by which
I will prove the facts clearly; although I know that you
remember what was done; I have still the fear that he
may be thought too insignificant a man to have done all
the evil which he has wrought—as indeed happened
before, when he caused the ruin of the unhappy Pho- | 346 B.C.
cians by the false report which he brought home. [143]
For the war at Amphissa which was the cause of Philip's
coming to Elateia, and of one being chosen commander
of the Amphictyons, who overthrew the fortunes of the
Hellenes—*he* it is who helped to get it up; he, in his sole | Philip
person, is to blame for disasters to which no equal can
be found. I protested at the time, and cried out, before | 339 B.C.
the Assembly, 'You are bringing war into Attica, Aeschines—an Amphictyonic War.' But a packed group of
his supporters refused to let me speak, while the rest

were amazed, and imagined that I was bringing a base-less charge against him, out of personal animosity. [144] But what the true nature of these proceedings was, men of Athens—why this plan was contrived, and how it was executed—you must hear from me to-day, since you were prevented from doing so at the time. You will behold a business cunningly organized; you will advance greatly in your knowledge of public affairs; and you will see what cleverness there was in Philip.

[145] Philip had no prospect of seeing the end of the war with you, or ridding himself of it, unless he could make the Thebans and Thessalians enemies of Athens. For although the war was being wretchedly and inefficiently conducted by your generals, he was nevertheless suffering infinite damage from the war itself and from the freebooters. The exportation of the produce of his country and the importation of what he needed were both impossible. [146] Moreover, he was not at that time superior to you at sea, nor could he reach Attica, if the Thessalians would not follow him, or the Thebans give him a passage through their country; and although he was overcoming in the field the generals whom you sent out, such as they were (for of this I say nothing), he found himself suffering from the geographical conditions themselves, and from the nature of the resources which either side possessed. [147] Now if he tried to encourage either the Thessalians or the Thebans to march against you in order to further his own quarrel, no one, he thought, would pay any attention to him; but if he adopted their own common grounds of action and were chosen commander, he hoped to find it easier to deceive or to persuade them, as the case might be. What then does he do? He attempts (and observe with what skill) to stir up an Amphictyonic War, and a disturbance in connexion with the meeting of the Council. [148] For he thought that they would at once find

that they needed his help, to deal with these. Now if one of his own or his allies' representatives on the Council brought the matter forward, he thought that both the Thebans and the Thessalians would regard the proceeding with suspicion, and that all would be on their guard: but if it was an Athenian, sent by you, his adversaries, that did so, he would easily escape detection —as, in fact, happened. How then did he manage this? He hired Aeschines. [149] No one, I suppose, either realized beforehand what was going on or guarded against it—that is how such affairs are usually conducted here; Aeschines was nominated a delegate to the Council; three or four people held up their hands for him, and he was declared elected. But when, bearing with him the prestige of this city, he reached the Amphictyons, he dismissed and closed his eyes to all other considerations, and proceeded to perform the task for which he had been hired. He composed and recited a story, in attractive language, of the way in which the Cirrhaean territory had come to be dedicated; [150] and with this he persuaded the members of the Council, who were unused to rhetoric and did not foresee what was about to happen, that they should resolve to make the circuit of the territory which the Amphisseans said they were cultivating because it was their own, while he alleged that it was part of the consecrated land. The Locrians were not bringing any suit against us, or taking any such action as (in order to justify himself) he now falsely alleges. You may know this from the following consideration. It was clearly impossible for the Locrians to bring a suit against Athens to an actual issue, without summoning us. Who then served the summons upon us? Before what authority was it served? Tell us who knows: point to him. You cannot do so. It was a hollow and a false pretext of which you thus made a wrongful use. [151] While the Amphictyons were mak-

Aeschines represents Athens at the Amphictyonic meeting, spring 339 B.C.

Compare Aeschines *Against Ctesiphon* §§107–29

Compare Aeschines §116

ing the circuit of the territory in accordance with Aeschines' suggestion, the Locrians fell upon them and came near to shooting them all down with their spears; some of the members of the Council they even carried off with them. And now that complaints and hostilities had been stirred up against the Amphisseans, in consequence of these proceedings, the command was first held by Cottyphus, and his force was drawn from the Amphictyonic Powers alone. But since some did not come, and those who came did nothing, the men who had been suborned for the purpose—villains of long standing, chosen from the Thessalians and from the traitors in other States—took steps with a view to entrusting the affair to Philip, as commander, at the next meeting of the Council. [152] They had adopted arguments of a persuasive kind. Either, they said, the Amphictyons must themselves contribute funds, maintain mercenaries, and fine those who refused to do so; or they must elect Philip. To make a long story short, the result was that Philip was appointed. And immediately afterwards, having collected a force and crossed the Pass, ostensibly on his way to the territory of Cirrha, he bids a long farewell to the Cirrhaeans and Locrians, and seizes Elateia. [153] Now if the Thebans had not changed their policy at once, upon seeing this, and joined us, the trouble would have descended upon the city in full force, like a torrent in winter. As it was, the Thebans checked him for the moment; chiefly, men of Athens, through the goodwill of some Heavenly Power towards us; but secondarily, so far as it lay in one man's power, through me also. (*To the clerk.*) Now give me the decrees in question, and the dates of each proceeding; (*to the jury*) that you may know what trouble this abominable creature stirred up, unpunished. (*To the clerk.*) Read me the decrees.

E.g., Athens; Aeschines §§125–29

Philip called in to Greece, 338 B.C.

A Phocian town that commands the road to Thebes and Athens

[154] [*The decrees of the Amphictyons are read.*]

(*To the clerk.*) Now read the dates of these proceedings. [155] (*To the jury.*) They are the dates at which Aeschines was delegate to the Council. (*To the clerk.*) Read.

[156]   [*The dates are read.*]

Now give me the letter which Philip sent to his allies in the Peloponnese, when the Thebans failed to obey his summons. For from this, too, you may clearly see that he concealed the real reason for his action— the fact that he was taking measures against Hellas and the Thebans and yourselves—and pretended to represent the common cause and the will of the Amphictyons. And the man who provided him with all these occasions and pretexts was Aeschines. (*To the clerk.*) Read.

[157]   [*Philip's letter is read.*]

[158] You see that he avoids the mention of his own reasons for action, and takes refuge in those provided by the Amphictyons. Who was it that helped him to prepare such a case? Who put such pretexts at his disposal? Who is most to blame for the disasters that have taken place? Is it not Aeschines? And so, men of Athens, you must not go about saying that Hellas has suffered such things as these at the hands of one man. I call Earth and Heaven to witness, that it was at the hands, not of one man, but of many villains in each State. And of these Aeschines is one; and, had I to speak the truth [159] without any reserve, I should not hesitate to describe him as the incarnate curse of all alike—men, regions or cities—that have been ruined since then. For he who supplied the seed is responsible for the crop. I

Philip

177

wonder that you did not turn away your eyes at the very sight of him: but a cloud of darkness seems to hang between you and the truth.

[160] I find that in dealing with the measures taken by Aeschines for the injury of his country, I have reached the time when I must speak of my own statesmanship in opposition to these measures; and it is fair that you should listen to this, for many reasons, but above all because it will be a shameful thing, if, when I have faced the actual realities of hard work for you, you will not even suffer the story of them to be told. [161] For when I saw the Thebans, and (I may almost say) yourselves as well, being led by the corrupt partisans of Philip in either State to overlook, without taking a single precaution against it, the thing which was really dangerous to both peoples and needed their utmost watchfulness—the unhindered growth of Philip's power; while, on the contrary, you were quite ready to entertain ill-feeling and to quarrel with one another; I kept unceasing watch to prevent this. Nor did I rely only on my own judgement in thinking that this was what your interest required. [162] I knew that Aristophon, and afterwards Eubulus, always wished to bring about this friendly union, and that, often as they opposed one another in other matters, they always agreed in this. Cunning fox! While they lived, you hung about them and flattered them; yet now that they are dead, you do not see that you are attacking them. For your censure of my policy in regard to Thebes is far more a denunciation of them than of me, since they were before me in approving of that alliance. [163] But I return to my previous point—that it was when Aeschines had brought about the war at Amphissa, and the others, his accomplices, had effectually helped him to create the ill-feeling against the Thebans, that Philip marched against us. For it was to render this possible that their attempt

Athenian
politicians,·
considered
pro-Theban

178

to throw the two cities into collision was made; and had we not roused ourselves a little before it was too late, we should never have been able to regain the lost ground; to such a length had these men carried matters. What the relations between the two peoples already were, you will know when you have heard these decrees and replies. (*To the clerk.*) Take these and read them.

[164, 165]   [*The decrees are read.*]

[166] (*To the clerk.*) Now read the replies.

[167]   [*The replies are read.*]

[168] Having established such relations between the cities, through the agency of these men, and being elated by these decrees and replies, Philip came with his army and seized Elateia, thinking that under no circumstances whatever should we and the Thebans join in unison after this. And though the commotion which followed in the city is known to you all, let me relate to you briefly just the bare facts.

[169] It was evening, and one had come to the Prytanes with the news that Elateia had been taken. Upon this they rose up from supper without delay; some of them drove the occupants out of the booths in the market-place and set fire to the wicker-work; others sent for the generals and summoned the trumpeter; and the city was full of commotion. On the morrow, at break of day, the Prytanes summoned the Council to the Council-Chamber, while you made your way to the Assembly; and before the Council had transacted its business and passed its draft-resolution, the whole people was seated on the hill-side. [170] And now, when the Council had arrived, and the Prytanes had reported the

The word of Philip's surprise move on Elateia reaches Athens, 338 B.C.

". . . by the
compression
of his
language he
has made us
imagine the
mood of the
time, and he
has embossed
his phrases
with the
uniqueness of
the disaster."
—Longinus

intelligence which they had received, and had brought forward the messenger, and he had made his statement, the herald proceeded to ask, 'Who wishes to speak?' But no one came forward; and though the herald repeated the question many times, still no one rose, though all the generals were present, and all the orators, and the voice of their country was calling for some one to speak for her deliverance. For the voice of the herald, uttered in accordance with the laws, is rightly to be regarded as the common voice of our country. [171] And yet, if it was for those to come forward who wished for the deliverance of the city, all of you and all the other Athenians would have risen, and proceeded to the platform, for I am certain that you all wished for her deliverance. If it was for the wealthiest, the Three Hundred would have risen; and if it was for those who had both these qualifications—loyalty to the city and wealth—then those would have risen, who subsequently made those large donations; for it was loyalty and wealth that led them so to do. [172] But that crisis and that day called, it seems, not merely for a man of loyalty and wealth, but for one who had also followed the course of events closely from the first, and had come to a true conclusion as to the motive and the aim with which Philip was acting as he was. For no one who was unacquainted with these, and had not scrutinized them from an early period, was any the more likely, for all his loyalty and wealth, to know what should be done, or to be able to advise you. The man who was needed was found that day in me. [173] I came forward and addressed you in words which I ask you to listen to with attention, for two reasons—first, because I would have you realize that I was the only orator or politician who did not desert his post as a loyal citizen in the hour of danger, but was found there, speaking and proposing what your need required, in the midst of the terror;

Compare
Aeschines
§§140–41

and secondly, because by the expenditure of a small amount of time, you will be far better qualified for the future in the whole art of political administration. [174] My words then were these: 'Those who are unduly disturbed by the idea that Philip can count upon the support of Thebes do not, I think, understand the present situation. For I am quite sure that, if this were so, we should have heard of his being, not at Elateia, but on our own borders. At the same time, I understand quite well, that he has come to prepare the way for himself at Thebes. [175] Listen,' I said, 'while I tell you the true state of affairs. Philip already has at his disposal all the Thebans whom he could win over either by bribery or by deception; and those who have resisted him from the first and are opposing him now, he has no chance of winning. What then is his design and object in seizing Elateia? He wishes, by making a display of force in their neighbourhood and bringing up his army, to encourage and embolden his own friends, and to strike terror into his enemies, that so they may either concede out of terror what they now refuse, or may be compelled. [176] Now,' I said, 'if we make up our minds at the present moment to remember any ill-natured action which the Thebans may have done us, and to distrust them on the assumption that they are on the side of our enemies, we shall be doing, in the first place, just what Philip would pray for: and further, I am afraid that his present opponents may then welcome him, that all may philippize with one consent, and that he and they may march to Attica together. If, however, you follow my advice, and give your minds to the problem before us, instead of to contentious criticism of anything that I may say, I believe that I shall be able to win your approval for my proposals, and to dispel the danger which threatens the city. What then must you do? [177] You must first moderate your present alarm,

Demosthenes'
advice

and then change your attitude, and be alarmed, all of you, for the Thebans. They are far more within the reach of disaster than we: it is they whom the danger threatens first. Secondly, those who are of military age, with the cavalry, must march to Eleusis, and let every one see that you yourselves are in arms; in order that those who sympathize with you in Thebes may be enabled to speak in defence of the right, with the same freedom that their opponents enjoy, when they see that, just as those who are trying to sell their country to Philip have a force ready to help them at Elateia, so those who would struggle for freedom have you ready at hand to help them, and to go to their aid, if any one attacks them. [178] Next I bid you elect ten envoys, and give them full authority, with the generals, to decide the time of their own journey to Thebes, and to order the march of the troops. But when the envoys arrive in Thebes, how do I advise that they should handle the matter? I ask your special attention to this.

Compare
Aeschines
§142

They must require nothing of the Thebans—to do so at such a moment would be shameful; but they must undertake that we will go to their aid, if they bid us do so, on the ground that they are in extreme peril, and that we foresee the future better than they; in order that, if they accept our offer and take our advice, we may have secured our object, and our action may wear an aspect worthy of this city; or, if after all we are unsuccessful, the Thebans may have themselves to blame for any mistakes which they now make, while we shall have done nothing disgraceful or ignoble.' [179] When I had spoken these words, and others in the same strain, I left the platform. All joined in commending these proposals; no one said a word in opposition; and I did

Compare
Aeschines
§145

not speak thus, and then fail to move a motion; nor move a motion, and then fail to serve as envoy; nor serve as envoy, and then fail to persuade the Thebans. I car-

ried the matter through in person from beginning to
end, and gave myself up unreservedly to meet the
dangers which encompassed the city. . . .

[188] This was the first step towards our new relations with Thebes, and the beginning of a settlement.
Up to this time the cities had been inveigled into mutual
hostility, hatred, and mistrust by these men. But this
decree caused the peril that encompassed the city to
pass away like a cloud. It was for an honest citizen,
if he had any better plan than mine, to make it public
at the time, instead of attacking me now. [189] The true
counsellor and the dishonest accuser, unlike as they are
in everything, differ most of all in this: the one declares
his opinion before the event, and freely surrenders himself as responsible, to those who follow his advice, to
Fortune, to circumstances, to any one. The other is
silent when he ought to speak, and then carps at anything untoward that may happen. [190] That crisis, as
I have said, was the opportunity for a man who cared
for his country, the opportunity for honest speaking.
But so much further than I need will I go, that if any
one can *now* point to any better course—or any course
at all except that which I chose—I admit my guilt. If
any one has discovered any course to-day, which would
have been for our advantage, had we followed it at
the time, I admit that it ought not to have escaped me.
But if there neither is nor was such a possibility; if even
now, even to-day, no one can mention any such course,
what was the counsellor of the people to do? Had he
not to choose the best of the plans which suggested
themselves and were feasible? [191] This I did. For
the herald asked the question, Aeschines, 'Who wishes
to speak?' not 'Who wishes to bring accusations about
the past?' nor 'Who wishes to guarantee the future?'
And while you sat speechless in the Assembly throughout that period, I came forward and spoke. Since, how-

Compare
Longinus
*On the
Sublime*,
chapter 39

ever, you did not do so then, at least inform us now, and tell us what words, which should have been upon my lips, were left unspoken, what precious opportunity, offered to the city, was left unused, by me? What alliance was there, what course of action, to which I ought, by preference, to have guided my countrymen?

[192] But with all mankind the past is always dismissed from consideration, and no one under any circumstances proposes to deliberate about it. It is the future or the present that make their call upon a statesman's duty. Now at that time the danger was partly in the future, and partly already present; and instead of cavilling disingenuously at the results, consider the principle of my policy under such circumstances. For in everything the final issue falls out as Heaven wills; but the principle which he follows itself reveals the mind of the statesman. [193] Do not, therefore, count it a crime on my part, that Philip proved victorious in the battle. The issue of that event lay with God, not with me. But show me that I did not adopt every expedient that was possible, so far as human reason could calculate; that I did not carry out my plan honestly and diligently, with exertions greater than my strength could bear; or that the policy which I initiated was not honourable, and worthy of Athens, and indeed necessary: and then denounce me, but not before. [194] But if the thunderbolt which fell has proved too mighty, not only for us, but for all the other Hellenes, what are we to do? It is as though a ship-owner, who had done all that he could to ensure safety, and had equipped the ship with all that he thought would enable her to escape destruction, and had then met with a tempest in which the tackling had been strained or even broken to pieces, were to be held responsible for the wreck of the vessel. 'Why,' he would say, 'I was not steering the ship'—just as I was not the general 'I had no power over Fortune:

Philip defeats Athens and Thebes at Chaeronea, 338 B.C.

Fortune

she had power over everything.' But consider and observe this point. [195] If it was fated that we should fare as we did, even when we had the Thebans to help us in the struggle, what must we have expected, if we had not had even them for our allies, but they had joined Philip?—and this was the object for which Philip employed every tone that he could command. And if, when the battle took place, as it did, three days' march from Attica, the city was encompassed by such peril and terror, what should we have had to expect, if this same disaster had occurred anywhere within the borders of our own country? Do you realize that, as it was, a single day, and a second, and a third gave us the power to rally, to collect our forces, to take breath, to do much that made for the deliverance of the city: but that had it been otherwise—it is not well, however, to speak of things which we have not had to experience, thanks to the goodwill of one of the gods, and to the protection which the city obtained for herself in this alliance, which you denounce.

[196] The whole of this long argument, gentlemen of the jury, is addressed to yourselves and to the circle of listeners outside the bar; for to this despicable man it would have been enough to address a short, plain sentence. If to you alone, Aeschines, the future was clear, before it came, you should have given warning, when the city was deliberating upon the subject; but if you had no such foreknowledge, you have the same ignorance to answer for as others. Why then should you make these charges against me, any more than I against you? [197] For I have been a better citizen than you with regard to this very matter of which I am speaking—I am not as yet talking of anything else—just in so far as I gave myself up to the policy which all thought expedient, neither shrinking from nor regarding any personal risk; while you neither offered any better proposals

than mine (for then they would not have followed mine),
nor yet made yourself useful in advancing mine in any
way. What the most worthless of men, the bitterest
enemy of the city, would do, you are found to have done,
when all was over; and at the same time as the irrecon-
cilable enemies of the city, Aristratus in Naxos, and
Aristoleos in Thasos, are bringing the friends of Athens
to trial, Aeschines, in Athens itself, is accusing Demosthenes. [198] But surely one who treasured up the
misfortunes of the Hellenes, that he might win glory
from them for himself, deserved to perish rather than
to stand as the accuser of another; and one who has
profited by the very same crisis as the enemies of the
city cannot possibly be loyal to his country. You prove
it, moreover, by the life you live, the actions you do, the
measures you take—and the measures, too, that you do
not take. Is anything being done which seems advantageous to the city? Aeschines is speechless. Has
any obstruction, any untoward event occurred? There
you find Aeschines, like a rupture or a sprain, which
wakes into life, so soon as any trouble overtakes the
body.

[199] But since he bears so hardly upon the results,
I desire to say what may even be a paradox; and let
no one, in the name of Heaven, be amazed at the length
to which I go, but give a kindly consideration to what
I say. Even if what was to come was plain to all beforehand; even if all foreknew it; even if you, Aeschines,
had been crying with a loud voice in warning and pro-
testation—you who uttered not so much as a sound; even
then, I say, it was not right for the city to abandon her
course, if she had any regard for her fame, or for our
forefathers, or for the ages to come. [200] As it is, she
is thought, no doubt, to have failed to secure her object—as happens to all alike, whenever God wills it: but
then, by abandoning in favour of Philip her claim to

take the lead of others, she must have incurred the blame of having betrayed them all. Had she surrendered without a struggle those claims in defence of which our forefathers faced every imaginable peril, who would not have cast scorn upon you, Aeschines—upon you, I say; not, I trust, upon Athens nor upon me? [201] In God's name, with what faces should we have looked upon those who came to visit the city, if events had come round to the same conclusion as they now have— if Philip had been chosen as commander and lord of all, and we had stood apart, while others carried on the struggle to prevent these things; and that, although the city had never yet in time past preferred an inglorious security to the hazardous vindication of a noble cause? [202] What Hellene, what foreigner, does not know, that the Thebans, and the Spartans, who were powerful still earlier, and the Persian king would all gratefully and gladly have allowed Athens to take what she liked and keep all that was her own, if she would do the bidding of another, and let another take the first place in Hellas? [203] But this was not, it appears, the tradition of the Athenians; it was not tolerable; it was not in their nature. From the beginning of time no one had ever yet succeeded in persuading the city to throw in her lot with those who were strong, but unrighteous in their dealings, and to enjoy the security of servitude. Throughout all time she has maintained her perilous struggle for pre-eminence, honour, and glory. [204] And this policy you look upon as so lofty, so proper to your own national character, that, of your forefathers also, it is those who have acted thus that you praise most highly. And naturally. For who would not admire the courage of those men, who did not fear to leave their land and their city, and to embark upon their ships, that they might not do the bidding of another; who chose for their general The-

Xerxes' offer
in 480 B.C.

The battle
of Salamis,
480 B.C.

An Athenian
who
counselled
submitting
to the
Persians

mistocles (who had counselled them thus), and stoned
Cyrsilus to death, when he gave his voice for submission
to a master's orders—and not him alone, for your wives
stoned his wife also to death. [205] For the Athenians
of that day did not look for an orator or a general who
would enable them to live in happy servitude; they
cared not to live at all, unless they might live in freedom. For every one of them felt that he had come into
being, not for his father and his mother alone, but also
for his country. And wherein lies the difference? He who
thinks he was born for his parents alone awaits the
death which destiny assigns him in the course of nature:
but he who thinks he was born for his country also will
be willing to die, that he may not see her in bondage,
and will look upon the outrages and the indignities
that he must needs bear in a city that is in bondage as
more to be dreaded than death.

> Demosthenes drives home his point that the policy
> which he advocated was a continuation of the
> best traditions of Athens, and then resumes his
> narrative:

The debate
in Thebes,
338 B.C.

[211] When we came to Thebes, we found envoys
there from Philip, and from the Thessalians and his
other allies—our friends in terror, his full of confidence.
And to show you that I am not saying this now to suit
my own purpose, read the letter which we, your envoys, dispatched without delay. [212] The prosecutor,
however, has exercised the art of misrepresentation to so
extravagant a degree, that he attributes to circumstances,
not to me, any satisfactory result that was achieved; but
for everything that fell out otherwise, he lays the blame
upon me and the fortune that attends me. In his eyes,
apparently, I, the counsellor and orator, have no share
in the credit for what was accomplished as the result of

oratory and debate; while I must bear the blame alone for the misfortunes which we suffered in arms, and as a result of generalship. What more brutal, more damnable misrepresentation can be conceived? (*To the clerk.*) Read the letter.

[*The letter is read.*]

[213] When they had convened the Assembly, they gave audience to the other side first, on the ground that they occupied the position of allies; and these came forward and delivered harangues full of the praises of Philip and of accusations against yourselves, recalling everything that you had ever done in opposition to the Thebans. The sum of it all was that they required the Thebans to show their gratitude for the benefits which they had received from Philip, and to exact the penalty for the injuries they had received from you, in whichever way they preferred—either by letting them march through their country against you, or by joining them in the invasion of Attica; and they showed (as they thought) that the result of the course which they advised would be that the herds and slaves and other valuables of Attica would find their way into Boeotia; while the result of what (as they alleged) you were about to propose would be that those of Boeotia would be plundered in consequence of the war. [214] They said much more, but all tending to the same effect. As for our reply, I would give my whole life to tell it you in detail; but I fear lest, now that those times have gone by, you may feel as if a very deluge had overwhelmed all, and may regard anything that is said on the subject as vanity and vexation. But hear at least what we persuaded them to do, and their answer to us. (*To the clerk.*) Take this and read it.

[*The answer of the Thebans is read.*]

[215] After this they invited and summoned you; you marched; you went to their aid; and (to pass over the events which intervened) they received you in so friendly a spirit that while their infantry and cavalry were encamped outside the walls, they welcomed your troops into their houses, within the city, among their children and wives, and all that was most precious to them. Three eulogies did the Thebans pronounce upon you before the world that day, and those of the most honourable kind—the first upon your courage, the second upon your righteousness, the third upon your self-control. For when they chose to side with you in the struggle, rather than against you, they judged that your courage was greater, and your requests more righteous, than Philip's; and when they placed in your power what they and all men guard most jealously, their children and wives, they showed their confidence in your self-control. [216] In all these points, men of Athens, your conduct proved that their judgement had been correct. For the force came into the city; but no one made a single complaint—not even an unfounded complaint—against you; so virtuously did you conduct yourselves. And twice you fought by their side, in the earliest battles—the battle by the river and the winter-battle—and showed yourselves, not only irreproachable, but even admirable, in your discipline, your equipment, and your enthusiasm. These things called forth expressions of thanks to you from other states, and sacrifices and processions to the gods from yourselves. [217] And I should like to ask Aeschines whether, when all this was happening, and the city was full of pride and joy and thanksgiving, he joined in the sacrifices and the rejoicing of the multitude, or whether he sat at home grieving and groaning and angry at the good fortune of

Preliminaries to Chaeronea, winter 339–38 B.C.

his country. If he was present, and was seen in his place with the rest, surely his present action is atrocious —nay, even impious—when he asks you, who have taken an oath by the gods, to vote to-day that those very things were not excellent, of whose excellence he himself on that day made the gods his witnesses. If he was not present, then surely he deserves to die many times, for grieving at the sight of the things which brought rejoicing to others. (*To the clerk.*) Now read these decrees.

[*The decrees ordering sacrifices are read.*]

[218] Thus we were occupied at that time with sacrifices, while the Thebans were reflecting how they had been saved by our help; and those who, in consequence of my opponents' proceedings, had expected that they would themselves stand in need of help, found themselves, after all, helping others, in consequence of the action they took upon my advice. But what the tone of Philip's utterance was, and how greatly he was confounded by what had happened, you can learn from his letter, which he sent to the Peloponnese. (*To the clerk.*) Take these and read them: (*to the jury*) that you may know what was effected by my perseverance, by my travels, by the hardships I endured, by all those decrees of which Aeschines spoke so disparagingly just now.

Compare
Aeschines
§§141–43

Demosthenes tells of the efforts he expended on Athens' behalf in the early 330's and the honors he received, a precedent, he contends, for Ctesiphon's motion. Then he turns to another point in Aeschines' case:

[227] Yes, and he ingeniously suggests that you ought to disregard the opinion which you had of each

of us when you left your homes and came into court; and that just as, when you draw up an account in the belief that some one has a balance, you nevertheless give way when you find that the counters all disappear and leave nothing over, so now you should give your adhesion to the conclusion which emerges from the argument. Now observe how inherently rotten everything that springs from dishonesty seems to be. [228] By his very use of this ingenious illustration he has confessed that to-day, at all events, our respective characters are well established—that I am known to speak for my country's good, and he to speak for Philip. For unless that were your present conception of each of us, he would not have sought to change your view. [229] And further, I shall easily show you that it is not fair of him to ask you to alter this opinion—not by the use of counters—that is not how a political reckoning is made—but by briefly recalling each point to you, and treating you who hear me both as auditors of my account and witnesses to the facts. For that policy of mine which he denounces caused the Thebans, instead of joining Philip, as all expected them to do, in the invasion of our country, to range themselves by our side and stay his progress. [230] It caused the war to take place not in Attica, but on the confines of Boeotia, eighty miles from the city. Instead of our being harried and plundered by freebooters from Euboea, it gave peace to Attica from the side of the sea throughout the war. Instead of Philip's taking Byzantium and becoming master of the Hellespont, it caused the Byzantines to join us in the war against him. [231] Can such achievements, think you, be reckoned up like counters? Are we to cancel them out, rather than provide that they shall be remembered for all time? I need not now add that it fell to others to taste the barbarity which is to be seen in every case in which Philip got any one finally into

Compare Aeschines' use of the abacus image, §59

Advantages of Demosthenes' policy

his power; while you reaped (and quite rightly) the fruits of the generosity which he feigned while he was bringing within his grasp all that remained. But I pass this over.

[232] Nay, I will not even hesitate to say, that one who wished to review an orator's career straightforwardly and without misrepresentation, would not have included in his charges such matters as you just now spoke of—making up illustrations, and mimicking words and gestures. Of course the fortune which befell the Hellenes—surely you see this?—was entirely due to my using this word instead of that, or waving my hand in one direction rather than the other! [233] He would have inquired, by reference to the actual facts, what resources and what forces the city had at her command when I entered political life; what I subsequently collected for her when I took control; and what was the condition of our adversaries. Then if I had diminished our forces, he would have proved that the fault lay at my door; but if I had greatly increased them, he would have abstained from deliberate misrepresentation. But since you have avoided such an inquiry, I will undertake it; and do you, gentlemen, observe whether my argument is just.

[234] The military resources of the city included the islanders—and not all, but only the weakest. For neither Chios nor Rhodes nor Corcyra was with us. Their contribution in money came to 45 talents, and these had been collected in advance. Infantry and cavalry, besides our own, we had none. But the circumstance which was most alarming to us and most favourable to our enemies was that these men had contrived that all our neighbours should be more inclined to enmity than to friendship—the Megareans, the Thebans, and the Euboeans. [235] Such was the position of the city at the time; and what I say admits of no contradiction. Now consider the position of Philip, with whom our conflict

lay. In the first place, he held absolute sway over his followers—and this for purposes of war is the greatest of all advantages. Next, his followers had their weapons in their hands always. Then he was well off for money, and did whatever he resolved to do, without giving warning of it by decrees, or debating about it in public, or being put on trial by dishonest accusers, or defending himself against indictments for illegality, or being bound to render an account to any one. He was himself absolute master, commander, and lord of all. [236] But I who was set to oppose him—for this inquiry too it is just to make—what had I under my control? Nothing! For, to begin with, the very right to address you—the only right I had—you extended to Philip's hirelings in the same measure as to me; and as often as they defeated me—and this frequently happened, whatever the reason on each occasion—so often you went away leaving a resolution recorded in favour of the enemy. [237] But in spite of all these disadvantages, I won for you the alliance of the Euboeans, Achaeans, Corinthians, Thebans, Megareans, Leucadians, and Corcyreans, from whom were collected—apart from their citizen-troops—15,000 mercenaries and 2,000 cavalry. [238] And I instituted a money-contribution, on as large a scale as I could. But if you refer, Aeschines, to what was fair as between ourselves and the Thebans or the Byzantines or the Euboeans—if at this time you talk to us of equal shares—you must be ignorant, in the first place, of the fact that in former days also, out of those ships of war, three hundred in all, which fought for the Hellenes, Athens provided two hundred, and did not think herself unfairly used, or let herself be seen arraigning those who had counselled her action, or taking offence at the arrangement. It would have been shameful. No! men saw her rendering thanks to Heaven, because when a common peril beset the Hellenes, she had provided double

Demosthenes' diplomatic efforts

Aeschines §143

Athens provided two-thirds of the ships at Salamis, 480 B.C.

as much as all the rest to secure the deliverance of all. [239] Moreover, it is but a hollow benefit that you are conferring upon your countrymen by your dishonest charges against me. Why do you tell them *now*, what course they ought to have taken? Why did you not propose such a course at the time (for you were in Athens, and were present) if it was possible in the midst of those critical times, when we had to accept, not what we chose, but what circumstances allowed; since there was one at hand, bidding against us, and ready to welcome those whom we rejected, and to pay them into the bargain.

[240] But if I am accused to-day, for what I have actually done, what if at the time I had haggled over these details, and the other states had gone off and joined Philip, and he had become master at once of Euboea and Thebes and Byzantium? What do you think these impious men would then have done? What would they have said? [241] Would they not have declared that the states had been surrendered? that they had been driven away, when they wished to be on your side? 'See,' they would have said (would they not?), 'he has obtained through the Byzantines the command of the Hellespont and the control of the corn trade of Hellas; and through the Thebans a trying border war has been brought into Attica; and owing to the pirates who sail from Euboea, the sea has become unnavigable,' and much more in addition. [242] A villainous thing, men of Athens, is the dishonest accuser always— villainous, and in every way malignant and fault-finding! Aye, and this miserable creature is a fox by nature, that has never done anything honest or gentlemanly— a very tragical ape, a clodhopping Oenomaus, a counterfeit orator! [243] Where is the profit to your country from your cleverness? Do you instruct us now about things that are past? It is as though a doctor, when he

Aeschines
once acted in
Sophocles'
Oenomaus

was paying his visits to the sick, were to give them no advice or instructions to enable them to become free from their illness, but, when one of his patients died and the customary offerings were being paid him, were to explain, as he followed to the tomb, 'if this man had done such and such things, he would not have died.' Crazy fool! Do you tell us this *now*?

[244] Nor again will you find that the defeat—if you exult at it, when you ought to groan, accursed man! —was determined by anything that was within my control. Consider the question thus. In no place to which I was sent by you as ambassador, did I ever come away defeated by the ambassadors of Philip—not from Thessaly nor from Ambracia, not from the Illyrians nor from the Thracian princes, not from Byzantium nor from any other place, nor yet, on the last occasion, from Thebes. But every place in which his ambassadors were defeated in argument, he proceeded to attack and subdue by force of arms. [245] Do you then require those places at *my* hands? Are you not ashamed to jeer at a man as a coward, and in the same breath to require him to prove superior, by his own unaided efforts, to the army of Philip—and that with no weapons to use but words? For what else was at my disposal? I could not control the spirit of each soldier, or the fortune of the combatants, or the generalship displayed, of which, in your perversity, you demand an account from me. [246] No; but every investigation that can be made as regards those duties for which an orator should be held responsible, I bid you make. I crave no mercy. And what are those duties? To discern events in their beginnings, to foresee what is coming, and to forewarn others. These things I have done. Again, it is his duty to reduce to the smallest possible compass, wherever he finds them, the slowness, the hesitation, the ignorance, the contentiousness, which are the errors inseparably connected

The function of the orator

with the constitution of all city-states; while, on the other hand, he must stimulate men to unity, friendship, and eagerness to perform their duty. All these things I have done, and no one can discover any dereliction of duty on my part at any time. [247] If one were to ask any person whatever, by what means Philip had accomplished the majority of his successes, every one would reply that it was by means of his army, and by giving presents and corrupting those in charge of affairs. Now I had no control or command of the forces: neither, then, does the responsibility for anything that was done in that sphere concern me. And further, in the matter of being or not being corrupted by bribes, I have defeated Philip. For just as the bidder has conquered one who accepts his money, if he effects his purchase, so one who refuses to accept it has conquered the bidder. In all, therefore, in which I am concerned, the city has suffered no defeat.

[248] The justification, then, with which I furnished the defendant for such a motion as he proposed with regard to me, consisted (along with many other points) of the facts which I have described, and others like them. I will now proceed to that justification which all of you supplied. For immediately after the battle, the People, who knew and had seen all that I did, and now stood in the very midst of the peril and terror, at a moment when it would not have been surprising if the majority had shown some harshness towards me—the People, I say, in the first place carried my proposals for ensuring the safety of the city; and all the measures undertaken for its protection—the disposition of the garrisons, the entrenchments, the funds for the fortifications—were all provided for by decrees which I proposed. And, in the second place, when the People chose a corn-commissioner, out of all Athens they elected me. [249] Subsequently all those who were interested in

Compare
Aeschines
§159

injuring me combined, and assailed me with indictments, prosecutions after audit, impeachments, and all
such proceedings—not in their own names at first, but
through the agency of men behind whom, they thought,
they would best be screened against recognition. For you
doubtless know and remember that during the early part
of that period I was brought to trial every day; and
neither the desperation of Sosicles, nor the dishonest
misrepresentations of Philocrates, nor the frenzy of
Diondas and Melantus, nor any other expedient, was left
untried by them against me. And in all these trials,
thanks to the gods above all, but secondarily to you
and the rest of the Athenians, I was acquitted—and
justly; for such a decision is in accordance both with
truth and with the credit of jurors who have taken their
oath, and given a verdict in conformity with it. [250] So
whenever I was impeached, and you absolved me and
did not give the prosecutor the necessary fraction of
the votes, you were voting that my policy was the best.
Whenever I was acquitted upon an indictment, it was a
proof that my motion and proposals were according to
law. Whenever you set your seal to my accounts at an
audit, you confessed in addition that I had acted
throughout with uprightness and integrity. And this
being so, what epithet was it fitting or just that Ctesiphon should apply to my actions? Was it not that which
he saw applied by the People, and by juries on their oath,
and ratified by Truth in the judgement of all men?

An excursus on Fortune provides Demosthenes
with an opportunity to compare his own education and life with Aeschines'. The result is some
of Demosthenes' choicest invective:

[256] If, however, you determine at all costs to
scrutinize my fortune, Aeschines, then compare it with
your own; and if you find that mine is better than yours,

then cease to revile it. Examine it, then, from the very
beginning. And, in Heaven's name, let no one condemn
me for any want of good taste. For I neither regard one
who speaks insultingly of poverty, nor one who prides
himself on having been brought up in affluence, as a man
of sense. But the slanders and misrepresentations of
this unfeeling man oblige me to enter upon a discussion
of this sort; and I will conduct it with as much moderation as the facts allow.

[257] I then, Aeschines, had the advantage as a boy
of attending the schools which became my position, and
of possessing as much as one who is to do nothing ignoble owing to poverty must possess. When I passed out
of boyhood, my life corresponded with my upbringing—
I provided choruses and equipped warships; I paid the
war-tax; I neglected none of the paths to distinction in
public or private life, but gave my services both to my
country and my friends; and when I thought fit to enter
public life, the measures which I decided to adopt were
of such a character that I have been crowned many
times both by my country and by many other Hellenic
peoples, while not even you, my enemies, attempt to
say that my choice was not at least an honourable one.
[258]. Such is the fortune which has accompanied my
life, and though I might say much more about it, I re-
frain from doing so, in my anxiety not to annoy any one
by the expression of my pride. And you—the lofty per-
sonage, the despiser of others—what has been your fortune when compared with this?—the fortune, thanks to
which you were brought up as a boy in the depths of
indigence, in close attendance upon the school along
with your father, pounding up the ink, sponging down
the forms, sweeping the attendants' room, occupying the
position of a menial, not of a free-born boy! [259]
Then, when you became a man, you used to read out
the books to your mother at her initiations, and help

The strange
rituals
presided
overy by
Aeschines'
mother

her in the rest of the hocus-pocus, by night dressing the
initiated in fawnskins, drenching them from the bowl,
purifying them and wiping them down with the clay and
the bran, and (when they were purified) bidding them
stand up and say, 'The ill is done, the good begun,'
priding yourself upon raising the shout of joy more
loudly than any one had ever done before—and I can
believe it, for, when his voice is so loud, you dare not
imagine that his shout is anything but superlatively fine.
[260]. But by day you used to lead those noble com-
panies through the streets, men crowned with fennel and
white poplar, throttling the puff-adders and waving
them over your head, crying out 'Euoe, Saboe,' and danc-
ing to the tune of 'Hyes Attes, Attes Hyes'—addressed by
the old hags as leader, captain, ivy-bearer, fan-bearer,
and so on; and as the reward of your services getting
sops and twists and barley buns! Who would not con-
gratulate himself with good reason on such things, and
bless his own fortune? [261] But when you were enrolled
among your fellow parishioners, by whatever means (for
of that I say nothing)—when, I say, you *were* enrolled,
you at once selected the noblest of occupations, that
of a clerk and servant to petty magistrates. [262] And
when at length you escaped from this condition also,
after yourself doing all that you impute to others, you
in no way—Heaven knows!—disgraced your previous
record by the life which you subsequently lived; for

You were an
actor in the
countryside
and lived
off the land

you hired yourself out to the actors Simylus and Socrates
—the Roarers, they were nicknamed—and played as a
third-rate actor, collecting figs and bunches of grapes
and olives, like a fruiterer gathering from other peoples'
farms, and getting more out of this than out of the dra-
matic competitions in which you were competing for
your lives; for there was war without truce or herald
between yourselves and the spectators; and the many
wounds you received from them make it natural for

you to jeer at the cowardice of those who have had no such experiences. [263] But I will pass over all that might be accounted for by your poverty, and proceed to my charges against your character itself. For you chose a line of political action (when at length it occurred to you to take up politics too), in pursuance of which, when your country's fortune was good, you lived the life of a hare, in fear and trembling, always expecting a thrashing for the crimes which lay on your conscience; whereas all have seen your boldness amid the misfortunes of others. [264] But when a man plucks up courage at the death of a thousand of his fellow citizens, what does he deserve to suffer at the hands of the living? I have much more to say about him, but I will leave it unsaid. It is not for me, I think, to mention lightly all the infamy and disgrace which I could prove to be connected with him, but only so much as it is not discreditable to myself to speak of.

[265] And now review the history of your life and of mine, side by side—good temperedly, Aeschines, not unkindly: and then ask these gentlemen which fortune, of the two, each of them would choose. You taught letters; I attended school. You conducted initiations; I was initiated. You were a clerk; I a member of the Assembly: you, a third-rate actor, I a spectator of the play. You used to be driven from the stage, while I hissed. Your political life has all been lived for the good of our enemies, mine for the good of my country [266]. To pass over all besides, even on this very day, I am being examined with regard to my qualification for a crown—it is already admitted that I am clear of all crimes; while you have already the reputation of a dishonest informer, and for you the issue at stake is whether you are to continue such practices, or to be stopped once for all, through failing to obtain a fifth part of the votes. A good fortune

Aeschines and Demosthenes compared

A prosecutor winning less than one-fifth of the votes is prohibited from further indictments.

indeed—can you not see?—is that which has accompanied your life, that you should denounce mine!

[267] And now let me read to you the evidence of the public burdens which I have undertaken; and side by side with them, do you, Aeschines, read the speeches which you used to murder—

Opening of
Euripides'
Hecuba

'I leave the abysm of death and gates of gloom' and 'Know that I am not fain ill-news to bring'; and 'evil in evil wise,' may you be brought to perdition, by the gods above all, and then by all those here present, villainous citizen, villainous third-rate actor that you are. (*To the clerk.*) Read the evidence.

> The contrast between his own career and Aeschines' soon leads Demosthenes into a discussion of the proper conduct of the orator. His own skill has always been directed towards the public good, while Aeschines has simply sought opportunities to display his clever rhetoric and elocution.

[280] Yet it is not his language, Aeschines, that deserves our esteem in an orator, nor the pitch of his voice, but his choice of the aims which the people chooses, his hatred or love of those whom his country loves or hates. [281] He whose heart is so disposed will always speak with loyal intent; but he who serves those from whom the city foresees danger to herself, does not ride at the same anchor as the People, and therefore does not look for safety to the same quarter. But I do, mark you! For I have made the interests of my countrymen my own, and have counted nothing as reserved for my own private advantage. [282] What? You have not done so either? How can that be, when immediately after the battle you went your way as an ambassador to Philip, the author of the calamities which befell your country at that time; and that, despite the fact that until then you always denied this intimacy with him,

as everyone knows? But what is meant by a deceiver of the city? Is it not one who does not say what he thinks? Upon whom does the herald justly pronounce the curse? Is it not upon such a man as this? With what greater crime can one charge a man who is an orator, than that of saying one thing and thinking another? Such a man you have been found to be. [283] And after this do you open your mouth, or dare to look this audience in the face? Do you imagine that they do not know who you are? or that the slumber of forgetfulness has taken such hold upon them all, that they do not remember the speeches which you used to deliver during the war, when you declared with imprecations and oaths that you had nothing to do with Philip, and that I was bringing this accusation against you, when it was not true, to satisfy my personal enmity? [284] But so soon as the news of the battle had come, you thought no more of all this, but at once avowed and professed that you stood on a footing of friendship and guest-friendship with him; though these were nothing but your hireling-service under other names; for upon what honest or equal basis could Aeschines, the son of Glaucothea the tambourine-player, enjoy the guest-friendship, or the friendship, or the acquaintance of Philip? I cannot see. In fact, you had been hired by him to ruin the interests of these your countrymen. And yet, though your own treason has been so plainly detected—though you have been an informer against yourself after the event—you still revile me, and reproach me with crimes of which, you will find, any one is more guilty than I.

Chaeronea

Compare §130

[285] Many a great and noble enterprise, Aeschines, did this city undertake and succeed in, inspired by me; and she did not forget them. It is a proof of this, that when, immediately after the event, the People had to elect one who should pronounce the oration over the dead, and you were nominated, they did not elect you,

After
Chaeronea,
Demosthenes
gave the
funeral
oration

for all your fine voice, nor Demades, who had just negotiated the Peace, nor Hegemon, nor any other member
of your party: they elected me. And when you and
Pythocles came forward in a brutal and shameless fashion, God knows! and made the same charges against
me as you are making again to-day, and abused me, the
People elected me even more decidedly. And the reason
you know well; but I will tell it you nevertheless. [286]
They knew for themselves both the loyalty and zeal
which inspired my conduct of affairs, and the iniquity of
yourself and your friends. For what you denied with
oaths when our cause was prosperous, you admitted in
the hour of the city's failure; and those, accordingly,
who were only enabled by the misfortunes of their
country to express their views without fear, they decided to have been enemies of their own for a long
while, though only then did they stand revealed. [287]
And further, they thought that one who was to pronounce an oration over the dead, and to adorn their
valour, should not have come beneath the same roof, nor
shared the same libation, as those who were arrayed
against them; that he should not there join with those
Compare
Aeschines
§152
who with their own hands had slain them, in the revel
and the triumph-song over the calamities of the Hellenes, and then come home and receive honour—that he
should not play the mourner over their fate with his
voice, but should grieve for them in his heart. What
they required they saw in themselves and in me, but
not in you; and this was why they appointed me, and
not any of you. [288] Nor, when the people acted thus,
did the fathers and brothers of the slain, who were
then publicly appointed to conduct the funeral, act
otherwise. For since (in accordance with the ordinary
custom) they had to hold the funeral-feast in the house
of the nearest of kin, as it were, to the slain, they held
it at my house, and with reason; for though by birth

each was more nearly akin to his dead than I, yet none stood nearer to them all in common. For he who had their life and their success most at heart, had also, when they had suffered what I would they had not, the greatest share of sorrow for them all.

(*To the clerk.*) Read him the epitaph which the city resolved to inscribe above them at the public cost; (*to Aeschines*) that even by these very lines, Aeschines, you may know that you are a man destitute of feeling, a dishonest accuser, an abominable wretch!

[*The Epitaph*]

> Demosthenes points out that the epitaph ascribes the defeat of the Athenians not to the failures of any statesman or to any other human cause but to the gods. Demosthenes thus holds himself blameless of the disaster while grouping Aeschines among a lengthy catalogue of traitors, profligates, and sycophants who exchanged the freedom and independence which earlier Greeks regarded as the embodiment of the good for the satisfaction of their basest appetites.

[297] Of this shameful and notorious conspiracy and wickedness—or rather (to speak with all earnestness, men of Athens), of this treason against the freedom of the Hellenes—Athens has been guiltless in the eyes of all men, in consequence of my statesmanship, as I have been guiltless in your eyes. And do you then ask me for what merits I count myself worthy to receive honour? I tell you that at a time when every politician in Hellas had been corrupted—beginning with yourself— [298] no opportunity that offered, no generous language, no grand promises, no hopes, no fears, nor any other motive, tempted or induced me to betray one jot of what I believed to be the rights and interests of the city; nor, of all the counsel that I have given to my fellow

Epilogue

countrymen, up to this day, has any ever been given (as it has by you) with the scales of the mind inclining to the side of gain, but all out of an upright, honest, uncorrupted soul. I have taken the lead in greater affairs than any man of my own time, and my administration has been sound and honest throughout all. [299] That is why I count myself worthy of honour. But as for the fortifications and entrenchments, for which you ridiculed me, I judge them to be deserving, indeed, of gratitude and commendation—assuredly they are so— but I set them far below my own political services. Not with stones, nor with bricks, did I fortify this city. Not such are the works upon which I pride myself most. But would you inquire honestly wherein my fortifications consist? You will find them in munitions of war, in cities, in countries, in harbours, in ships, in horses, and in men ready to defend my fellow countrymen. [300] These are the defences I have set to protect Attica, so far as by human calculation it could be done; and with these I have fortified our whole territory—not the circuit of the Peiraeus or of the city alone. Nor in fact, did *I* prove inferior to Philip in calculations—far from it! —or in preparations for war; but the generals of the confederacy, and their forces, proved inferior to him in fortune. Where are the proofs of these things? They are clear and manifest. I bid you consider them.

[301] What was the duty of a loyal citizen—one who was acting with all forethought and zeal and uprightness for his country's good? Was it not to make Euboea the bulwark of Attica on the side of the sea, and Boeotia on that of the mainland, and on that of the regions towards the Peloponnese, our neighbours in that direction? Was it not to provide for the corn-trade, and to ensure that it should pass along a continuously friendly coast all the way to the Peiraeus? [302] Was it not to preserve the places which were ours—Procon-

nesus, the Chersonese, Tenedos—by dispatching expeditions to aid them, and proposing and moving resolutions accordingly; and to secure the friendship and alliance of the rest—Byzantium, Tenedos, Euboea? Was it not to take away the greatest of the resources which the enemy possessed, and to add what was lacking to those of the city? [303] All this has been accomplished by my decrees and by the measures which I have taken; and all these measures, men of Athens, will be found by any one who will examine them without jealousy, to have been correctly planned, and executed with entire honesty: the opportunity for each step was not, you will find, neglected or left unrecognized or thrown away by me, and nothing was left undone, which it was within the power and the reasoning capacity of a single man to effect. But if the might of some Divine Power, or the inferiority of our generals, or the wickedness of those who were betraying your cities, or all these things together, continuously injured our whole cause, until they effected its overthrow, how is Demosthenes at fault? [304] Had there been in each of the cities of Hellas one man, such as I was, as I stood at my own post in your midst—nay, if all Thessaly and all Arcadia had each had but one man animated by the same spirit as myself—not one Hellenic people, either beyond or on this side of Thermopylae, would have experienced the evils which they now suffer. [305] All would have been dwelling in liberty and independence, free from all fears, secure and prosperous, each in their own land, rendering thanks for all these great blessings to you and the rest of the Athenian people, through me. But that you may know that in my anxiety to avoid jealousy, I am using language which is far from adequate to the actual facts, (*to the clerk*) read me this; and take and recite the list of the expeditions sent out in accordance with my decrees.

The reason
for our failure

In a staccato of short sentences Demosthenes
asserts that Aeschines has been totally useless to
the state—speaking only to upset, contributing
nothing to the war effort, and totally abandoning
the city's traditions. He then summarizes his own
accomplishments:

[321] Two characteristics, men of Athens, a citizen
of a respectable character (for this is perhaps the least
invidious phrase that I can apply to myself) must be
able to show: when he enjoys authority, he must maintain to the end the policy whose aims are noble action
and the pre-eminence of his country: and at all times
and in every phase of fortune he must remain loyal. For
this depends upon his own nature; while his power and
his influence are determined by external causes. And
in me, you will find, this loyalty has persisted unalloyed.
[322] For mark this. Not when my surrender was demanded, not when I was called to account before the
Amphictyons, not in face either of threats or of promises, not when these accursed men were hounded on
against me like wild beasts, have I ever been false to
my loyalty towards you. For from the very first, I chose
the straight and honest path in public life: I chose to
foster the honour, the supremacy, the good name of my
country, to seek to enhance them, and to stand or fall
with them. [323] I do not walk through the market,
cheerful and exultant over the success of strangers, hold-
ing out my hand and giving the good tidings to any
whom I expect to report my conduct yonder, but shud-
dering, groaning, bowing myself to the earth, when I
hear of the city's good fortune, as do these impious men,
who make a mock of the city—not remembering that in
so doing they are mocking themselves—while they direct their gaze abroad, and, whenever another has
gained success through the failure of the Hellenes, be-

laud that state of things, and declare that we must see that it endures for all time.

[324] Never, O all ye gods, may any of you consent to their desire! If it can be, may you implant even in these men a better mind and heart. But if they are verily beyond all cure, then bring them and them alone to utter and early destruction, by land and sea. And to us who remain, grant the speediest release from the fears that hang over us, and safety that naught can shake!

Peroration

THE FUNERAL ORATION OF HYPERIDES

INTRODUCTION

The funeral oration by Hyperides with which this volume concludes is the last preserved speech of a major Attic orator. Delivered in 322 B.C. at the public funeral of the Athenians who had died in the campaigns of that year, it honored the Athenian casualties in the war against Macedon which was set off by the news of Alexander's death (323 B.C.). The bold confidence that with the death of the Macedonian leader the control which that kingdom exercised over Greece could also be removed soon gave way to the recognition that the Greek states, even with a leader as able as Leosthenes, could not achieve the cooperation and commitment necessary to win back their complete autonomy. The war was short and unspectacular; the principal episode was the siege of the Thessalian town Lamia from which the war takes its name. By late 322 it was clear that Macedon could not be resisted. The settlement which followed the Lamian War was far more severe than that reached after Chaeronea. A garrison was installed in the Peiraeus and the anti-Macedonian agitators were to be turned over. By the end of the year the two most prominent opponents of Macedon had died, Hyperides at the hands of Macedonian executors, Demosthenes by taking poison.

Thus this speech marks not only the end of Athens' role as a major power, but also the close of her greatest period of oratory. The following centuries never again saw the full excellence of Attic rhetoric. Yet, at the same time a new age was beginning whose outlines can sometimes be faintly glimpsed in the passages of this oration discovered in the last century buried among the long-abandoned remains of an Egypt that was once Greek.

The text printed here is J. O. Burtt's translation of the papyrus and of a passage found in a late classical anthology which probably was originally part of the conclusion of the speech. In square brackets are added certain transitions that represent the probable sequence of thought in places where the text of the papyrus is mutilated. Other important gaps in the papyrus are indicated by three dots.

––––––––––

[1] The words to be pronounced above this grave, a tribute to Leosthenes the general and the others who have perished with him in the war, for the courage they have shown, have as their witness time itself [which holds the record of their deeds. For no man known during the history of the world has seen in any land a nobler choice than this] nor better men than these now dead nor more resplendent actions. [2] Indeed my greatest doubt today is lest my speech may prove unworthy of their exploits. I am, however, taking heart in this assurance: that what I leave unsaid will be supplied by you who hear me; for my listeners will be no random audience but the persons who themselves have witnessed the actions of these men. [3] While praise is due to Athens for her policy, for choosing as she did a course not only ranking with her past achievements but even surpassing them in pride and honour, and to the fallen also for their gallantry in battle, for proving worthy of their forbears' valour, to Leosthenes the general it is doubly due; the city's guide in framing her decision, he was besides the citizens' commander in the field.

Proem
§§1–3

[4] In the case of Athens, to recount in detail the benefits which she has previously conferred upon the whole of Greece would be a task too great to compass in the time we have, nor is the occasion one for lengthy speaking. Indeed it is not easy for a single man, faced

Past accomplishments of Athens
§4 and 5

with so many noble actions, to recall the full story to your minds. I shall, however, venture one general comment on her. [5] Compare her with the sun which visits the whole world and duly separates the seasons, disposing all things for the best, with provision, where men are virtuous and prudent, for their birth and nurture, the crops and all the other needs of life; for so our city never fails to punish the wicked, help the just, mete out to all men fairness in place of wrong, and at her individual peril and expense assure the Greeks a common safety. [6] To deal with the achievements of the city as a whole is, as I said before, a task which I shall not attempt, and I will here confine myself to Leosthenes and his companions. At what point, then, shall I take up the story? What shall I mention first? Shall I trace the ancestry of each? To do so would, I think, be foolish. [7] Granted, if one is praising men of a different stamp, such as have gathered from divers places into the city which they inhabit, each contributing his lineage to the common stock, then one must trace their separate ancestry. But from one who speaks of Athenians, born of their own country and sharing a lineage of unrivalled purity, a eulogy of the descent of each must surely be superfluous. [8] Am I then to touch upon their education, and, as other speakers often do, remind you how as children they were reared and trained in strict self-discipline? None of us, I think, is unaware that our aim in training children is to convert them into valiant men; and that men who have proved of exceptional courage in war were well brought up in childhood needs no stressing. [9] The simplest course, I think, will be to tell you of their courage under arms, revealing them as authors of many benefits conferred upon their country and the rest of Greece. First I shall take the general, as is his due. [10] For Leosthenes perceived that the whole of Greece was humiliated and

Accomplishments of Leosthenes and his men §§6–26

Their paideia

Their courage

... cowed, corrupted by men who were accepting bribes from Philip and Alexander against their native countries. He realized that our city stood in need of a commander, and Greece herself of a city, able to assume the leadership, and he gave himself to his country and the city to the Greeks, in the cause of freedom. [11] After raising a mercenary force he took command of the citizen army and defeated the first opponents of Greek freedom, the Boeotians, Macedonians and Euboeans, together with their other allies, in battle in Boeotia. Thence he advanced to Pylae and occupied the pass through which, in bygone days as well, barbarians marched against the Greeks. He thus prevented the inroad of Antipater into Greece, and overtaking him in that vicinity, defeated him in battle and shut him into Lamia, which he then besieged [13] The Thessalians, Phocians, Aetolians, and all the other peoples of the region, he made his allies, bringing under his control, by their own consent, the men whom Philip and Alexander gloried in controlling against their wish. The circumstances subject to his will he mastered, but fate he could not overpower. [14] Leosthenes must have first claim upon our gratitude for ever, not only for the acts performed by him, but also for the later battle, fought after his death, and for those other triumphs which the Greeks have gained in this campaign. For on the foundations laid by Leosthenes the subsequent success of his survivors rests. [15] Let no one fancy that I disregard the other citizens and keep my eulogy for him alone. The praise bestowed upon Leosthenes for these engagements is in fact a tribute to the rest. For though sound strategy depends upon the leader, success in battle is ensured by those who are prepared to risk their lives; and therefore, in the praise that I bestow upon the victory gained, I shall be commending not merely the leadership of Leosthenes but the courage of his comrades too. [16] For who could

i. Leosthenes
§§10–14

ii. The others
§§15–26

213

rightly grudge his praise to those of our citizens who fell in this campaign, who gave their lives for the freedom of the Greeks, convinced that the surest proof of their desire to guarantee the liberty of Greece was to die in battle for her? [17] One circumstance did much to reinforce their purpose as champions of Greece: the fact that the earlier battle was fought in Boeotia. They saw that the city of Thebes had been tragically annihilated from the face of the earth, that its citadel was garrisoned by the Macedonians, and that the persons of its inhabitants were in slavery, while others parcelled out the land among themselves. And so these threats, revealed before their eyes, gave them an undaunted courage to meet danger gladly.

[18] Yet the action fought near Pylae and Lamia has proved to be as glorious for them as the conflict in Boeotia, not solely through the circumstances of victory in the field, over Antipater and his allies, but on the grounds of situation also. The fact that this has been the battle's site will mean that all the Greeks, repairing twice a year to the council of the Amphictyones, will witness their achievements; for by the very act of gathering in that spot they will recall the valour of these men. [19] Never before did men strive for a nobler cause, either against stronger adversaries or with fewer friends, convinced that valour gave strength and courage superiority as no mere numbers could. Liberty they gave us as an offering for all to share, but the honour of their deeds they have bestowed upon their country as a wreath for her alone.

[20] Now we might well reflect what, in our opinion, the outcome would have been, had these men failed to do their duty in the struggle. Must we not suppose that the whole world would be under one master, and Greece compelled to tolerate his whim as law? In short that Macedonian arrogance, and not the power of jus-

335 B.C.

The
Amphictyony
met at
Thermopylae

tice, would lord it among every people. . . . [21] The practices which even now we have to countenance are proof enough: sacrifices being made to men; images, altars, and temples carefully perfected in their honour, while those of the gods are neglected, and we ourselves are forced to honour as heroes the servants of these people. [22] If reverence for the gods has been removed by Macedonian insolence, what fate must we conclude would have befallen the rules of conduct towards man? Would they not have been utterly discounted? The more terrible therefore we think the consequences would have been, the greater must be the praise which we believe the dead have earned. [23] For no campaign has better shown the courage of the soldiers than this last, when they had daily to be arrayed for combat, to fight, on but one expedition, more battles than the combats which any soldier of the past endured, and face extreme severities of weather and many hard privations in the daily needs of life with an endurance almost beyond description.

[24] Such trials Leosthenes induced the citizens to brave undaunted and they gave up their persons gladly to share the struggle with so great a leader. Should they not then be counted fortunate in their display of valour rather than unfortunate in their sacrifice of life? For in exchange for a mortal body they gained undying glory, safeguarding by their personal courage the universal liberty of Greece. . . . [25] [Nothing brings complete happiness without self-government.] If men are to be happy, the voice of law, and not a ruler's threats, must reign supreme; if they are free, no groundless charge, but only proof of guilt, must cause them apprehension; nor must the safety of our citizens depend on those who slander them and truckle to their masters but on the force of law alone. [26] Such were the aims with which these men accepted labour upon labour, and with the

dangers of the passing hour dispelled the terrors which the whole future held for citizens and for Greeks, sacrificing their lives that others might live well.

Consolation
§§27–40

[27] To them we owe it that fathers have grown famous, and mothers looked up to in the city, that sisters, through the benefit of law, have made, and will make, marriages worthy of them, that children too will find a passport to the people's hearts in these men's valour; these men who, far from dying—death is no word to use where lives are lost, as theirs were, for a noble cause—have passed from this existence to an eternal state [28] For if the fact of death, to others a most grievous ill, has brought to them great benefits, are we not wrong indeed to count them wretched or to conclude that they have left the realm of life? Should we not rather say they have been born anew, a nobler birth than the first? Mere children then, they had no understanding, but now they have been born as valiant men. [29] Formerly they stood in need of time and many dangers to reveal their courage; now, with that courage as a base, they have become known to all, to be remembered for their valour. [30] On what occasion shall we fail to recollect the prowess of these men, in what place fail to see them win their due of emulation and the highest praise? What if the city prospers? Surely the successes, which they have earned, will bring their praises, and none other's, to our lips and to our memories. Shall we then forget them in times of personal satisfaction? We cannot; for it is through their valour that we shall have the safe enjoyment of those moments. [31] Will there be men of any age who will not count them blessed? What of the older generation, who think that through the efforts of these men they have been placed in safety and will pass the rest of their lives free from dread? Consider their compeers. [To them it has been given, because these died in battle, to enjoy their

i. Immortality

ii. Fame

lives in honour and safety.] Think too of the younger men and boys. [32] Will they not envy their death and strive themselves to take as an example these men's lives, in place of which they have left behind their valour? [33] Ought we then to count them happy in so great an honour? . . .

[34] . . . For it is for pleasure that men recall such feats of courage, what could be more pleasing to Greeks than the praise of those who gave them freedom from the Macedonian yoke? Or if it is desire for profit that prompts such recollections, what speech could be of greater profit to the hearts of those about to hear it than one which is to honour courage and brave men?

[35] With us and all mankind, it is clear, in the light of these reflections, that their fame is now assured, but what of the lower world? Who, we may well ask ourselves, are waiting there to welcome the leader of these men? Are we not convinced that we should see, greeting Leosthenes with wonder, those of the so-called demi-gods who sailed against Troy: heroes whom he so far excelled, though his exploits were akin to theirs, that they with all Greece at their side took but one city, while he with his native town alone brought low the whole power which held Europe and Asia beneath its sway? [36] They championed one lone woman wronged, but he staved off from all Greek women the violence coming upon them, aided by these men who now are being buried with him. [37] Remember the figures who, born after the heroes of old, yet rivalled their deeds of valour, the followers of Miltiades and Themistocles, and those others who, by freeing Greece, brought honour to their country and glory to their lives; [38] whom Leosthenes so far outdid in bravery and counsel, that where they beat back the barbarian power as it advanced, he even forestalled its onslaught.

Comparison with the heroes of the Trojan war

and of the Persian Wars

They saw a struggle with the foe in their own land, but he defeated his opponents on the foe's own soil.

The
tyrannicides
of 514 B.C.

[39] Those two, I fancy, who gave the people the surest token of their mutual friendship, Harmodius and Aristogiton, do not regard [any others more highly than] Leosthenes and his comrades in arms; nor are there any with whom they would rather hold converse in the lower world than these. We need not wonder; for what these men did was no less a task than theirs; it was indeed, if judgement must be passed, a greater service still. These two brought low the tyrants of their country, these the masters of the whole of Greece. [40] Noble indeed beyond our dreams was the courage these men attained, honourable and magnificent the choice they made. How supreme was the valour, the heroism in times [of peril, which they, dedicating to the universal liberty of Greece . . . .

> Here the papyrus breaks off. Part of the ending of the speech is quoted by Stobaeus, an anthologist of the fifth century A.D.:

Summary
§§41–43

[41] It is hard no doubt to offer consolation to those borne down with griefs like these. For sorrows are not stilled by word or law; only the individual's temper, and the measure of his feeling for the dead, can set the limit to his mourning. Yet we must take heart, and restricting our grief as best we may, bear in our minds, with the thought of death, the glorious name which the fallen have left behind them. [42] For though their fate deserves our tears, their conduct claims the highest praise. Though they have failed to reach old age in life, they have achieved a fame which knows no age, and have attained the height of satisfaction. For all who were childless at their death the praises of the Greeks will be immortal children. For all who have children alive the goodwill of their country will be the children's guard-

ian. [43] And furthermore, if death means non-existence, they have been released from sickness and from grief, and from the other ills which vex our human life. But if in Hades we are conscious still and cared for by some god, as we are led to think, then surely those who defended the worship of the gods, when it was being overthrown, must receive from him the greatest care of all. . . .

SUGGESTIONS FOR FURTHER READING

There is a great wealth of material by and about the
Attic orators now available in English. The principal
speeches have all been translated in the Loeb Classical
Library. A general survey of the development of Attic
oratory can be found in R. C. Jebb's old but still valuable handbook *The Attic Orators from Antiphon to
Isaeus* (2 volumes, London, 1876). More recently
George Kennedy has surveyed the techniques of Greek
oratory in a succinct and interesting study *The Art of
Persuasion in Greece* (Princeton, 1963). This supplements but cannot replace the understanding of ancient
oratory that can come from the study of treatises and
handbooks written by the Greeks themselves. The most
famous of these is Aristotle's *Rhetoric,* translated by
J. H. Freese for the Loeb Library, but in many ways
the so-called "Rhetoric to Alexander," falsely ascribed
to Aristotle, is more revealing. This has been translated
by H. Rackham for the Loeb series.

The historical background of the fourth century is
probably best set forth in J. B. Bury's *History of Greece*
(third edition, revised by R. Meiggs, London, 1959),
though the *Cambridge Ancient History* and M.L.W.

Laistner's *History of the Greek World from 479 to 323 B.C.* (London, 1936) also provide useful assistance.

Plutarch's life of Demosthenes, now available in a number of translations, is a delightful ancient sketch of the orator, though far from an adequate biography. Werner Jaeger's Sather lectures published under the title *Demosthenes* (Berkeley, 1938) help fill this need. The same scholar's *Paideia: The Ideals of Greek Culture* (3 volumes, translated by G. Highet, New York, 1945) is illuminating on ancient oratory, as it is on practically every aspect of the classical world. Philip of Macedon still lacks an adequate and sympathetic treatment in English, but his son Alexander is the subject of a fascinating, if controversial, biography by W. W. Tarn (*Alexander the Great*, Boston, 1956).

Finally two small volumes call attention to the continuing influence of the ancient orators, C. D. Adams' *Demosthenes and His Influence* (New York, 1927) and Georges Clemenceau's *Demosthenes* (translated by C. M. Thompson, Boston, 1926).

CHRONOLOGICAL TABLE

490 B.C.	Defeat of the Persians at Marathon
480	Defeat of the Persians at Salamis
479	Defeat of the Persians at Plataea
477	Formation of the Delian League; beginning of Athenian dominance
±459	Birth of Lysias
436	Birth of Isocrates; Athenian colony sent to Amphipolis
431-404	Peloponnesian War
405	Sparta destroys Athenian fleet at Aegospotami; beginning of Spartan dominance
403	Restoration of democracy in Athens
401-399	Expedition of Cyrus (Xenophon's *Anabasis*)
399	Death of Socrates
395-387	Corinthian War (Athens, Thebes and Corinth vs. Sparta); Lysias' *Funeral Oration*
394	Defeat of Spartan navy off Cnidus
390	Cyprus revolts from Persia; birth of Aeschines?
389	Birth of Hyperides
386	King's Peace

384	Birth of Demosthenes
±380	Death of Lysias; Isocrates' *Panegyricus*
377	Foundation of the second Athenian Confederacy
376	Athens defeats Sparta at the battle of Naxos
371	Thebes defeats Sparta at Leuctra; beginning of Theban dominance
362	Death of Theban leader Epaminondas
359	Philip becomes king of Macedon
358	Artaxerxes III becomes king of Persia
357	Athens and Macedon dispute over Amphipolis
356	Birth of Alexander the Great; outbreak of hostilities between Athens and Macedon
354	Demosthenes' first preserved speech
353	Athens keeps Philip from entering central Greece
351	Philip's Thracian expedition; Demosthenes' *Philippic* I
349	Philip moves against Chalcidice; Demosthenes' *Olynthiacs*
346	Peace of Philocrates; Isocrates' *Address to Philip*
344	Demosthenes' *Philippic* II
343	Dispute over Halonnesus
341	Athens sends Diopeithes to oppose Philip; Demosthenes' *Philippic* III
340	*Letter of Philip;* Philip's siege of Byzantium; outbreak of war between Athens and Macedon

SELECTED ANN ARBOR PAPERBACKS

works of enduring merit

For a complete list of Ann Arbor Paperback titles write:

THE UNIVERSITY OF MICHIGAN PRESS / ANN ARBOR